THE ILLUSTRATED GUIDE TO
ARMAGEDDON

BRITAIN'S COLD WAR

BOB CLARKE

Foreword by Steve Ladd, Colonel USAF (Retired), DFC

AMBERLEY PUBLISHING

First published 2012

Amberley Publishing Plc
The Hill, Stroud
Gloucestershire, GL5 4EP

www.amberley-books.com

Copyright © Bob Clarke 2012

The right of Bob Clarke to be identified as the Authors
of this work has been asserted in accordance with the Copyrights,
Designs and Patents Act 1988.

ISBN 978 1 4456 0915 7

British Library Cataloguing in Publication Data.
A catalogue record for this book is available from the British Library.

Typeset in 10pt on 13pt Celeste.
Typesetting by Amberley Publishing.
Printed in the UK.

CONTENTS

ACKNOWLEDGEMENTS

A number of people have had a hand in the development of this work and deserve mention beyond picture credits. In no particular order they are: Kev Knight, Ian Mullan, Eddie Doyle, Phil Harris, John Scofield, Gary Dagnall, Chris Jones, Andrew Law, Ian Lewis, Tony Maas, Teresa Thomas, Martin Bowman for the cover images as well as Neville Cullingford of the Royal Observer Corps Museum, United States Department of Defense Imagery Team, *Scarborough Evening News.*

A special thanks to Steve Ladd who wrote such a fantastic foreword and Campbell McCutcheon who continues to entertain my 'off-the-wall' ideas. In fact the list could, arguably, be endless and naturally there are likely to be those we have missed. If so I apologise in advance. As is now traditional I must mention Sarah, Alice and Hannah who have seen the fruits of six of these now and are, I am sure, looking forward to the next with glee!

FOREWORD

When Bob Clarke asked me to write the foreword to *The Illustrated Guide to Armageddon* my first thought was that it would be a pleasant undertaking and perhaps I could add a scrap of first-hand experience here and there, which might add something to the message he was conveying. As I read the manuscript, however, it became obvious that the scope of the book defined my formative years in so many separate ways that turning each page brought back a flood of memories. Granted, for the most part I grew up on the other side of 'the Pond' and my youthful Cold War-related experiences varied to some extent from those Bob has so vividly depicted in this volume; nevertheless we Yanks joined you in the anxiety, the paranoia and, yes, the occasional exhilaration of going head to head day after day and year after year with the dreaded (and now it seems overrated) Russian Bear. I now clearly recall the radio frequencies we were to tune to when the mushroom clouds filled the skies: '640/1240 Conelrad' (Control of Electromagnetic Radiation) and joining my young colleagues in crawling under our school desks in preparation for 'the Big One'. I can also remember the disappointment I felt when the Russkies beat us by putting that tiny silver ball with antennae in orbit first in 1957 – and followed up with Yuri Gagarin's orbital flight in 1961. We were, for that brief moment, losing the Space Race and in my adolescent mind, the end of the World was nigh.

Like most everyone else on the planet, I held my breath, seemingly for days on end, when US Intelligence identified offensive missiles en route to neighbouring Cuba, JFK confronted Khrushchev with the evidence, and we teetered on the brink of the unthinkable. For me, the crisis was close to home: my Dad was an Air Force officer stationed in the Pentagon War Room and he didn't ring or come home for the better part of a week. That wasn't like Dad – we were keenly aware that something truly monumental was brewing, and that it wasn't good.

As we all know, 'the other guy blinked', the Cuban Crisis ended, and tensions receded; I went off to university and then followed my Dad into the Air Force where I managed to qualify as a fighter pilot. Off to battle the Red Peril – 204 missions in Southeast Asia led to subsequent assignments in Spain and the UK and re-acquaintance with the Cold War scenarios that Bob has depicted so comprehensively in this book. Whilst references to QRA are most often evocative of heavy bomber forces, we did it too – whilst based at RAF Bentwaters in the F4 Phantom. Loaded centreline with a single B61 Y3 – a sleek, highly polished thermonuclear weapon with an impressive mahogany nosecone which fronted an airburst radar – we were capable of delivering 345 kilotons of fiery destruction to various military bases and industrial complexes in eastern Europe and the Soviet Union should the fabled balloon go up. The sensation of immense power that accompanied this capability was somewhat tempered by two factors: first, due to the fuel load of the Phantom and the distance to our assigned targets, we were acutely conscious that our trip, should it ever occur, would most certainly be one-way. Secondly, Intelligence gleefully informed us that we would be, at best, the third or fourth strike on any given target behind a plethora of the Army's Pershing missiles and the Strategic Air Command's finest. The faint glimmer of good news here was the fact that, whilst on QRA, we were equipped with one eye patch per crewman and highly reflective, gold-tinted helmet visors designed to reflect the radiant energy from dozens of nuclear blasts along our route enabling us to avoid blindness long enough to deliver our 'silver bullet'. We were less than totally convinced about the odds of this being successful, but then again we were young and fiercely dedicated to our mission. Every three months or so, we 'Certified' our detailed plan to obliterate individual targets to a panel consisting of the Wing's Weapons, Tactics and Navigation Officers and presided over by one of our resident Colonels. They grilled us on target details, expected defences, route and contingency issues, weapons and delivery settings and (much to our amusement) egress, escape and evasion plans. The final question at each of these Certifications was delivered by the aforementioned Colonel and invariably summarised the limiting factors above: 'Captain Ladd, let's suppose you successfully reach your target and find it to be a large smoking hole. What are you going to do?' There was only one correct answer: 'I'll make it a bigger smoking hole, Sir!' The Colonel was happy, I passed my Cert and the eight of us on the QRA hook that week went back to the Ready Room, watched old cowboy movies and hoped the klaxon wouldn't go off for real. Thankfully, it never did.

In 1979, the speed, noise and awesome power of the F4 was replaced (for me at least) by manoeuvrability, the whine of twin turbofans, and a seven-barrelled Gatling gun that unleashed 30mm rounds with impressive accuracy at a rate of seventy per second. Never mind that the A-10 Warthog looked ponderous and ungraceful, it was just what the West needed to counter the very real threat of a large scale Soviet armoured incursion into West Germany. When we first started flying her in East Anglia, a distraught woman near the Holbeach Gunnery range on the Wash rang the 81st TFW Command Post to complain: 'I don't know what it was, but it was big and gray, flying very low and it had two dustbins on the back!' Our RAF liaison officer, bless him, asked her if it had red stars on the wings. When she said no, he responded, 'Then thank your God, Madam,' and put the phone down. Once again, the complexion of the Cold War was evolving.

In very short order, Bentwaters/Woodbridge became the largest Fighter Wing in the world, operating 108 A-10s from the home 'drome and four Forward Operating Locations (FOLs) fanned out from north to south in close proximity to the Intra-German border (IGB), lending credence to the adage, 'You can't base A-10s near a swamp – the frogs will try to mate with them.' Again, I was in the right place at the right time (no skill or cunning involved) and served both as the Operations Officer at our Noervenich FOL near Düsseldorf and later as the Wing's OC Operations back at Bentwaters. Our mission, should we decide to accept it (or not!),

Above left: A Hot War interlude – Ubon Royal Thai Air Force Base, 1969. The Phantom's loaded with 500lb general-purpose bombs (on your left) and CBU 24 cluster bombs – 665 tennis ball-sized bomblets in a handy clamshell case – not a favourite of the Viet Cong for obvious reasons.

Middle: Same general-purpose bombs, but this time with fuse extenders – fused to detonate about waist level. It was seriously unhealthy to be strolling in the vicinity of impact. The difference between the bombs and the Smith and Wesson .38 combat special on my hip? I knew how to use the bombs.

Above right: Steve Ladd, Colonel USAF (Retired), DFC

was to provide a capable deterrent to the massive Soviet/GDR build-up of armoured forces. We trained near the border, familiarising our pilots with the anticipated area of operations. In the early days, the Warthog was 'technologically challenged', having nothing in the way of sophisticated navigational systems – a significant drawback for an airplane designed to operate at or below 100ft. Nevertheless, young pilots with plastic covered maps and a stopwatch quickly became adept at poking their noses ever closer to the border whilst avoiding the dreaded Air Traffic Control 'Brass Monkey' transmission on emergency frequencies which heralded a violation of the Central European Buffer Zone. With the help of our Luftwaffe colleagues at Noervenich, we once strapped a B61 onto a wing pylon of the obviously non-nuclear-capable A-10, took a photo of it and sent it, with a Christmas card, to the Commander of the Soviet Fourth Guards Tank Army, directly opposite us on the east side of the border. He never responded, but we hoped with all our hearts that his intelligence section was losing sleep over the revelation that their most formidable adversary might actually be able to vaporise them. Such was the chess game that was played out constantly between potential adversaries. Ten years later, the Berlin Wall was torn down through the combined efforts, over forty-five years, of hundreds of thousands of Brits, Americans, French, Germans, Belgians, Dutch, Scandinavians and many, many others.

As I look back, I am proud to be a very small part of that enormous evolution, and Bob Clarke's efforts in cataloguing the sights, sounds and events of a very special era were the catalyst that brought those memories back for me. If you were also a 'Baby Boomer' or in other ways a 'Child of the Cold War' I have no doubt this book will have the same effect on you. If not, it will give you a valuable insight into a fascinating period in history. Bob Clarke's *Armageddon* is an absorbing study of near-catastrophic confrontation between two incongruent cultures which could not have co-existed forever. The photographs within and the accompanying descriptions paint a vivid portrait of a mistrustful, edgy world and, indeed, provide some comfort that we, for all our faults, are capable of some extraordinary diplomacy, logic, and great restraint.

Steve Ladd, Colonel USAF (Retired), DFC

Chapter I

INTRODUCTION TO ARMAGEDDON

War is a complicated thing. By the start of the twentieth century it had become more than just facing armies, dragging, instead, entire populations into the maelstrom. The Second World War consumed over sixty million lives in just six years, a good number of them, over two thirds in fact, civilian. War is also recognisable. Images from the first fifty years of the twentieth century have shaped the way we view conflict and interpret world events with a hitherto unprecedented level of clarity. From the desolation of the battlefields of Northern France in the First World War to the death camps of Eastern Europe in the 1940s, a multitude of images guide us in our pursuit of understanding the concept of human savagery.

Post-Second World War conflict becomes less well defined, due in part to the nature of the Cold War. Granted, imagery played a major part in how the 'Eastern Bloc' and 'Free World' viewed each other, but to the British public the Cold War was punctuated by very few classic views – save perhaps the 'Golf Balls' at Fylingdales, the mushroom cloud or, during the 1980s, the rise in civil disobedience portrayed around the security fence at RAF Greenham Common. The ideological struggle that subsumed Super Power politics for forty years, however, was a ready source of propaganda through bias reporting and visual statements. A nice early example being Berliners waving at British and American transport aircraft during the Soviet blockade of the city, examples also include: the Korean War, napalm being used on supposed civilian targets in Vietnam, the Soviet invasion of Afghanistan on Christmas Day 1979 and subsequent struggle with CIA-equipped Mujahadine fighters and the boycotting of the Moscow (1980) and Los Angeles Olympics (1984) by Western and Eastern Bloc countries. Once you start the list is endless! Interestingly, international events feature far more readily in the British psyche than home-grown ones. Ask anyone born before 1960 what typifies the Cold War for them and more often than not it is events surrounding the Berlin Wall. That fascinates me, especially since the majority of the United Kingdom was on the front line – Intermediate Ballistic Missiles based across the Warsaw Pact made sure of it.

So why an *Illustrated Guide to Armageddon*? Well, first and foremost I wish to state that this book does not contain a deep political analysis of the facets of the Cold War, nor does it set out to furnish the world with a new set of 'iconic' images. The primary intent is to open up the Cold War for those who actually lived through it using, where possible, images that demonstrate some of the lesser-known aspects. And for those from later generations I have enlisted the help of my daughter Alice who is currently reading the period at school in the hope that this selection may be of use to those studying the Cold War. I was pleased that Steve Ladd wrote the foreword as he has placed the Cold War and his time in Britain into a global context. Remember, for NATO forces the UK was a posting overseas!

So what's included here? Successive British Governments had planned, from the outset of the Berlin Airlift, to protect the civilian population from air and, later, nuclear attack. However, by 1968 this had been downgraded to just civil servants, ministers and key personnel capable of coordinating the reconstruction of the country. What that protection, pre- and post-1968, was is presented in the following pages. The Government spent billions of pounds sterling on weapons systems and in so doing unwittingly provided some of the iconic shapes of the latter twentieth century, the Avro Vulcan being just one example. Some of these shapes will feature in this work. The intention is to show you what the Cold War actually looked like in Britain. From the well-meaning but ineffective Civil Defence Corps to the Air Defence of the Country, which incidentally got quite a workout through the 1970s and 1980s. As to where the government would hide itself if the Air Defence network failed and Soviet aircraft entered British airspace ... well, pretty much every site linked with the perpetuation of Government is now known. Some are impressive, well-thought-out structures, however, the majority are no more than basements. When the government assured us that:

'Most senior ministers, government officials, and service chiefs would have to remain at their desks if war threatened, and they would take their chance like anybody else if the UK were attacked.'

'Civil Defence – Why We Need It' (1981)

it seems they were being, by and large, honest. Unfortunately, little survives, if indeed it was ever recorded, of bunkers actually in use or on exercise. As you thumb through the many illustrations covering how the United Kingdom hoped to keep the invader from its shores, I would like you to ask yourself the following few questions: If the services I take for granted suddenly and without warning ceased what would I do to keep warm in winter? Where is the closest drinkable water supply? What does fourteen days' worth of food look like? Could I bury my children after watching them die from the effects of radiation poisoning? The last question is just as valid as the preceding three. Ultimately it was the two Super Powers' reluctance to go head to head that saved the population of Britain having to answer those and many other, more searching, questions. For other countries where the Cold War was fought, often by proxy, only the question of radiation remains unanswered; unfortunately burying children has not.

Opposite left: The trenches of Northern France epitomise the public's view of the First World War. Here an American Marine receives first aid in a trench on the Toulon Sector of the line in France. The conditions and horrors endured by all servicemen on the Western Front scarred the very fabric of society for decades after. The war also forced countries such as the United Kingdom to seek unilateral disarmament through the League of Nations until the mid-1930s. The photograph was taken by Sgt Leon H. Caverly, USMC on 22 March 1918. (Department of Defense Imagery photo no. HD-SN-99-02325)

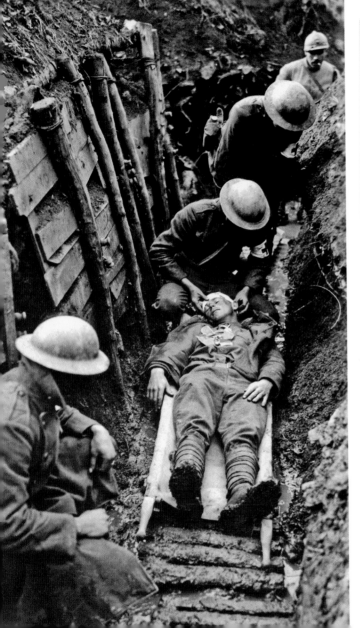

Above: Of the millions of images captured during the Second World War those surrounding the concentration camps continue to haunt the memory of the twentieth century. And so it was little wonder that when the Communist states on the Continent began to disintegrate and the practice of religious segregation again resurfaced, the world was horrified. The policy of 'Ethnic Cleansing' across the former Yugoslavia in the early 1990s had many governments drawing parallels with the camps of the 1930s and 1940s.

Right: The author describes the role of the United Kingdom Warning and Monitoring Organisation during a recent television interview.

Chapter 2

PERSONALITIES AND TIMELINES

To understand the Cold War and how it affected the United Kingdom some key international events need to be placed in context. Most readers will be familiar with the Berlin Wall, but when was it built and why? Likewise, the Cuban Missile Crisis or Korean War are both recognisable today and both had an effect on Britain, but when were they? This chapter introduces you to some of the key players and international events that had a major influence on Britain, especially defence spending, throughout the Cold War period.

Old Beginnings

First and foremost the Cold War was, to all intent and purpose, a struggle of ideologies; the socialist ideals of the Soviet Union and the capitalist movement in the West. Each had their merits, equally each had their flaws and in the case of socialism it was a big one – the dictatorial nature of how the socialist ideals of Marx and Engels (*The Communist Manifesto*, 1848) were interpreted. In October 1917, Leon Trotsky's Red Guards stormed the Winter Palace in Petrograd and in so doing altered the course of the whole of the twentieth century. By 1919, Soviet Leader Lenin had prophesied 'it is inconceivable that the Soviet Republic should continue for a long period side by side with imperialist states. Ultimately one or the other must conquer.' That same year a war-weary Western world intervened in the Russian Civil War and lost to the newly formed Red Army. Churchill later noted that the failure of the venture meant the West failed 'to strangle Bolshevism at birth'. The intervention warned the communist leadership that Western democracies would not tolerate the existence of a socialist state in their midst. Clearly if the revolution were to succeed then the Soviet Union needed to be militaristically strong.

When Lenin died in 1924, his successor Joseph Stalin pulled away from the idea of spreading communism beyond the Soviet border, focusing instead on a series of five year plans to build up the existing state. These were cut short by the Nazi invasion in mid-1941. Losses were staggering: at least 25 million Soviet citizens had perished by mid-1945. However, as a direct result, Stalin now commanded one of the two strongest military machines on the planet. The collapse of the Third Reich left a power vacuum across most of central and eastern Europe, Stalin simply took advantage of this and refused to leave many of the states he had 'liberated' from the Nazis. On 5 March 1946 Winston Churchill observed:

> From Stettin in the Baltic to Trieste in the Adriatic an iron curtain has descended across the Continent. Behind that line lie all the capitals of the ancient states of Central and Eastern Europe. Warsaw, Berlin, Prague, Vienna, Budapest, Belgrade, Bucharest and Sofia; all these famous cities and the populations around them lie in what I must call the Soviet sphere, and all are subject, in one form or another, not only to Soviet influence but to a very high and, in some cases, increasing measure of control from Moscow.

That 'measure of control' was to last until 1989 when Mikhail Gorbachev began, maybe unwittingly, but considered increasingly not so, the chain of events that eventually consumed the Soviet Union itself.

Vladimir Ilyich Lenin and Joseph Stalin, purported to be taken in Gorki, 1922. After the Bolshevik Revolution of November 1917 Lenin stated: 'We shall now proceed to construct the socialist order.' In so doing he threatened all other nation states, especially those who were still monarchist or democratic. From 1924 Stalin followed a more cautious path building up the Soviet Union's arsenal until, in 1947, the 'Trial of Strength', first prophesied by Hitler a few years earlier, developed.

Soviet War Memorial at Tiergarten, Berlin. The monument, one of several in the Berlin area, was constructed in the latter part of 1945 utilising stone from the Reich Chancellery. When Berlin was divided by the Allies the monument lay within the British Sector. Intended to make the city's population recognise Soviet losses, especially those in the Battle of Berlin, locally it became known as 'The Tomb of the Unknown Looter'. The Soviets kept an almost constant ceremonial guard on the monument throughout the Cold War, enforcing their right of travel in the Western Sectors. A similar situation surrounded the prison at Spandau, again in the British Sector, where Nazi war criminals were kept until the death of Rudolf Hess, the last inmate, in 1987.

The New World Order. When the leaders of the 'Big Three' met at the Potsdam Conference from 16 July–2 August 1945 the war in Europe was already over. President Harry S. Truman (centre) was considering using the atomic bomb in the Japanese theatre, mentioning being in possession of a 'powerful new weapon' to the Soviet leader. However, Stalin (right), through the espionage of Klaus Fuchs, a British scientist and Soviet sympathiser, had known about the device longer than Truman. Just eighteen months later the US President introduced a set of principles to Congress known as the Truman Doctrine. He called for the 'support of free peoples who are resisting attempted subjugation by armed minorities or by outside pressures'; the Second World War alliance was officially dead. Newly-elected British Prime Minister Clement Attlee is seated on the left.

The Marshall Plan, 5 June 1947. By late 1946, it was recognised that for there to be any chance of successful economic reconstruction and recovery the whole of Europe, especially Germany, would need vast amounts of external aid. In June 1947, the US Government launched the European Recovery Programme, widely known as the 'Marshall Plan', offering aid to any country who wanted it, including those who were still occupied by Soviet Forces. Naturally, Stalin refused on behalf of all the Central European states that were now behind the 'Iron Curtain'.

Above: The formation of NATO, 4 April 1949. Convinced by the Berlin Blockade that the Soviet Union would not relinquish its grip on the Central European states and of the comparative military weakness of western European countries, the American Government sought to bolster up their defences. On 4 April 1949 twelve countries formed the North Atlantic Treaty Organisation – NATO. An attack on one member country would now be an attack on all.

Left: The Berlin Blockade, 24 June 1948–12 May 1949, and Airlift, 25 June 1948–30 September 1949. On 20 June 1948, the Deutschmark was introduced as the new currency unit for the Western Zones of Germany. The Soviets had been warning against this from January as they realised its introduction would signal the end of reunifying the country and their aspirations for a communist Germany. Four days later surface routes to the city were closed and on 25 June the first of 2,300,000 tons of supplies were flown in by Allied civil and military aircraft. The blockade lasted until 12 May 1949.

Mao Tse-tung. For two decades the Chinese Communists struggled with the Kuomintang Party for control of the country. In 1947, the situation suddenly swung in the Communists' favour. On 1 October 1949, after a number of audacious battles, the Communists, led by Mao Tse-tung, announced the formation of the People's Republic of China. Stalin was surprised at the Communist victory, and alarmed, as this was a different interpretation of the words of Marx. More importantly, the Red Army and Moscow had had no hand in creating the new communist state and subsequent relations between the two giant neighbouring states were rocky throughout the Cold War.

The Korean War, 25 June 1950–23 July 1953. A T-34 tank on a bridge destroyed by a UN Forces airstrike. On 25 June 1950, the communist-controlled North Korea, under Kim Il-Sung, launched a surprise attack on its southern neighbour. The North Koreans were armed with Soviet T-34 tanks, Yak fighter aircraft and Soviet military advisors. Four days later the United Nations Security Council condemned the attack. The United States committed forces to the area the same day with the United Kingdom following suit a month later. ((Army) NARA FILE: 111-C-6143 WAR & CONFLICT BOOK: 1499)

Opposite left: Hungary, 1956. In mid-October 1956 Hungarian students began the most serious challenge to Soviet authority to date. Soviet troops with tanks sealed off the city and the growing rebellion was quashed. Imre Nagy was placed in charge and troops withdrew to the border on 28 October. Two days later Nagy declared an end to the one-party system; on 1 November, the government cabled the UN asking that Hungarian neutrality be considered. This was too much for Khrushchev and fifteen Soviet army divisions and 4,000 tanks crossed into the country on 3 November. The fighting lasted two weeks before the rising was finally crushed.

Opposite right: Fidel Castro. In January 1959, the '26 July Movement', led by Castro, finally forced the collapse of dictator General Batista's regime in Cuba. He immediately set about confiscating American-owned businesses and reducing the US Government's influence in the island state. The regime was not outwardly communist, however. Continued interference from Washington, including the disastrous 'Bay of Pigs' invasion by Batista exiles, drove Cuba closer to Moscow. In October 1962, the alliance would drive the world to the brink of nuclear war. (Library of Congress Prints and Photographs Division Washington, DC 20540)

Right: Francis Gary Powers, 1 May 1960. Francis Gary Powers' U-2 spy plane was shot down by a surface-to-air missile whilst deep in Soviet territory. He survived and was sentenced to ten years in prison. However, he was exchanged in Berlin twenty-one months later. The incident created an all-time low in Soviet-US relations. In Britain it forced an entire re-think of the Royal Air Force's plans to bomb Soviet targets. The Vulcan and other strike aircraft could no longer rely on height to keep them out of harm's way as Powers' U-2 had been at an altitude of 23,000+ metres when hit.

The Berlin Wall, 13 August 1961–9 November 1989. For nearly two decades, people, many of them skilled, had fled across the almost invisible border that divided the city of Berlin. Once it was clear the western powers had no intention of leaving the city, the East German authorities moved to stem the flow out of the country. The Anti-Fascist defence, as it was promoted in the east, was the brainchild of Erich Honecker, later leader of the DDR. The Berlin Wall became the symbol of a divided Europe, the epitome of Churchill's 'Iron Curtain'.

Soviet and American tanks face each other at Checkpoint Charlie, Berlin 27–28 October 1961. The four occupying forces in Berlin had unrestricted access into each other's administrative areas. That was until the US Chief of Mission in West Berlin, E. Allan Lightner, was stopped in his car at Checkpoint Charlie. By the evening of 27 October, both superpowers had deployed tanks in the city with ten from each side 'facing off' at the border control point. By 11 o'clock the following day, both NATO and Strategic Air Command were on full alert. This was the only time Soviet and American tanks faced each other in the entire Cold War.

John F. Kennedy meets Nikita Krushchev in Vienna, 4 June 1961. This was the first time both leaders had met. Khrushchev tried to bully the young and relatively inexperienced president into relinquishing Berlin. Kennedy refused and the talks, initially hailed as a success, set both superpowers on the road to the permanent partition of Europe and the Cuban Missile Crisis. Kennedy was assassinated on 22 November 1963 and Krushchev was ousted from power in October 1964 due to his reckless belligerence on the world stage.

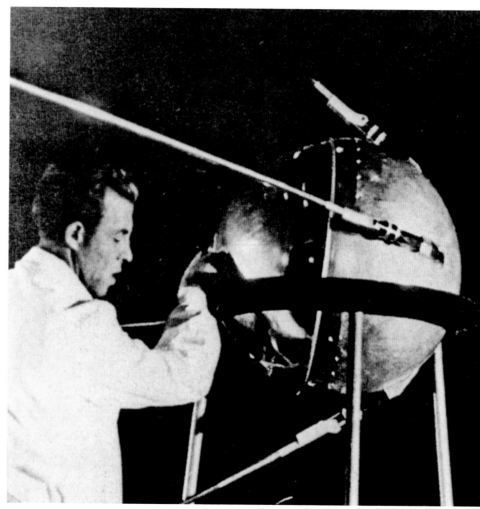

Above: Ivy Mike, 1 November 1952. Ivy Mike was the first fusion (hydrogen) device to be successfully detonated by the United States. The device, seen here, weighed in at 82 tons, partially due to a large refrigeration plant needed to keep liquid deuterium below 23.5 Kelvin. Within nine months, the Soviet Union had tested an air-deliverable device. The Soviet test prompted Winston Churchill to describe the unfolding situation as a 'delicate balance of terror'.

Right: Sputnik, 4 October 1957. Publicly credited as winning the first round of the 'space race', the world's first satellite, Sputnik, signalled not just the Soviets' superiority in rocketry but America's vulnerability to ballistic missiles. On 12 April 1961, Soviet Cosmonaut Yuri Gagarin became the first man in space.

Leonid Brezhnev, seen here with Tito (centre) in Moscow during a state visit, became First Secretary on 15 October 1964, initially sharing power with Andrei Kosygin (Prime Minister). Brezhnev's power base relied on a strong economy. However, increases in military expenditure, intended to keep parity with the US, and prestige projects like the space programme ensured the standard of living across the Soviet Union was well below western levels. Brezhnev's major achievement was the signing of the Strategic Arms Limitation Treaty (SALT) with Richard Nixon in 1972 and the policy of *Détente* that ensued throughout the 1970s.

Prague, Spring 1968. At the beginning of 1968 the Czechoslovakian administration began a series of reforms specifically aimed at decentralising the failing economy. Leonid Brezhnev met with the Czech leader, Alexander Dubcek, on 3 August demanding he stop the reforms at once. Seventeen days later, 500,000 Warsaw Pact troops poured over the border, crushing the hopes of millions. The West protested but had no way of intervening. (© Vldimir Lammer, Wenceslas Square, Prague, 1968)

Alexander Solzhenitsyn. The subject of human rights, or the lack of them, was one area where the West had the moral high ground. Throughout the Presidency of Jimmy Carter (1976–1980) human rights became a major area of concern, especially the treatment of authors. Solzhenitsyn had spent eleven years in a labour camp after the Second World War and continued to write about political imprisonment after his release. In 1974, the KGB discovered a manuscript for the book *Gulag Archipelago*, stripped Solzhenitsyn of Soviet citizenship and exiled him. Others were not so lucky and spent years in prison

The Vietnam War, 1965–1975. Throughout 1961–1964, Washington had been covertly increasing the number of military advisors in South Vietnam. Their purpose was to train the local force in anti-insurgency tactics against the communist Viet Cong raiding from the north of the country. By the time the last contingent of American troops left Vietnam, over 60,000 had died. The financial repercussions of the war in Vietnam meant a slowdown in funding for NATO, the removal of much of the ammunition stored in the United Kingdom, and forced the policy of *Détente* between the US and the Soviets.

Afghanistan, 1979–1989. On Christmas Day, 1979, huge numbers of Soviet infantry and tanks rolled over the border into Afghanistan. President Carter, in the State of the Union address a few weeks later, talked of nuclear weapons being an option but there was no need. The resilience of local fighters such as those pictured here (Sayyaf group Mujahedeen in Jaji, Paktia, Afghanistan, August 1984), ensured that the Red Army encountered stiff, mobile and often impossible-to-detect resistance. The adventure damaged two Olympic Games through boycotts and demonstrated the lack of direction the Soviet Union had in international affairs.

Solidarity, 1981. Throughout the 1970s the Polish economy, dependent on the West for many imports, was in crisis. The continual round of food price increases eventually led to mass strikes. From 14 August 1980, the country was at a standstill and the strikers, sensing something important was happening, formed Solidarity (Solidarnosc), which was within a year to have ten million members. Its leader, Lech Walesa, was eventually imprisoned along with thousands of others as the government declared martial law, but, in 1989, the Government was forced to negotiate and held semi-free elections.

Margaret Thatcher & Ronald Reagan. In May 1979 the Conservatives, under Margaret Thatcher, swept to power. Her Government immediately set about implementing a new Home Defence policy, incorporating a complete refurbishment of the bunker system around the United Kingdom. On the world stage she was formidable, earning the name the 'Iron Lady' from the Soviet Premier. Eighteen months later, Ronald Reagan was elected US President. Both leaders found a common resolve to face communism square on and set the scene for the eventual collapse of the Soviet system.

Pope John Paul II. Elected in 1978, Pope John Paul was instrumental in the rising of Solidarity in Poland. In 1979 he visited his home country where an estimated one in four of the population saw him during his nine-day stay. The arrival of the Pope awakened the Polish people, giving them a renewed self-confidence in both religion and politics. This message spread across Central European states, starting an undercurrent of resistance that was to end with the breaching of the Berlin Wall. (© *L'Osservatore Romano*)

Mikhail Gorbachev and Ronald Reagan, Geneva 1985. Gorbachev took office on the evening of 10 March 1985. By then, three Soviet premiers had died in as many years, so young blood (he was only fifty-four) was welcome. On meeting Reagan, on 19 November, he denounced the aging President as 'a cave man and a dinosaur'. By the end of the summit both men were talking arms control. In January 1986, Gorbachev offered to rid the Soviet Union of all nuclear weapons by 2000; now it would be the US administration that dragged its heels. (Courtesy of The Ronald Reagan Museum at Eureka College)

Gorbachev visits China, 15–18 May 1989. A four-day summit between China and the Soviet Union to open up a new dialogue between the two communist giants was hailed a success by both parties. Actually it sparked a massacre. Students, mindful of Gorbachev's requests for reform elsewhere, took the opportunity to mark his visit with a huge protest rally in Tiananmen Square. It was rumoured that Deng Xiaoping would resign; instead he waited until the Soviet delegation had left and then sent in the tanks. The number of dead remains unquantified; NATO suggests 7,000 whilst Amnesty International put it at nearer 1,000.

Checkpoint Charlie, 14 November 1989. West German children applaud as an East German couple drive through the checkpoint to take advantage of relaxed travel restrictions. The reunification of Germany was to take place eleven months later; by then the euphoria had been replaced with grave misgivings. The economic dream that was West Germany evaporated as it was discovered manufacturing and economic conditions over the border were some of the worst in the world. (Department of Defense Imagery photo no. DF-ST-91-01399)

Romania, 21 December 1989. Change swept the Continent throughout late 1989 as communist governments fell in quick succession. Surprisingly, most were without bloodshed. Even the East Germans, who had demonstrated a ready willingness to shoot escapees, did nothing. However, in Romania it was to be different. During a public address broadcast live on television, the Romanian President Nicolai Ceausescu was booed and whistled. The secret police eventually opened fire on the crowd, whilst the army sided with the demonstrators. Four days of fighting ensued. On 25 December 1989, Ceausescu and his wife were executed by firing squad.

Chapter 3

DEFENDING THE REALM

Throughout the Cold War, the United Kingdom maintained a massive military machine. That machine was diverse to say the least, often with equipment well beyond its intended retirement date. In fact, some weapons were defending the British mainland, the Bloodhound anti-aircraft missile being one such example, for the entire period of the Warsaw Pact threat. This section of the *Illustrated Guide to Armageddon* concerns itself with the defensive and offensive posture of the British Government through the Ministry of Defence.

Air Defence

A key element of British Cold War defence was the ability to detect approaching aircraft and co-ordinate an appropriate response to that threat. Radar, extensively developed during the Second World War, was the backbone of this air defence network. A number of ambitious plans were initiated over the years and practically all were either obsolete or rendered ineffective by Soviet countermeasures almost as soon as they came on line. Indeed, it is radar and other detection methods that so typifies the point that the Cold War was as much a war of science and technology as anything else.

Throughout the late 1940s and early 1950s, British air defence comprised a number of recognisable components. They were the radar stations around the coast that could detect enemy aircraft approaching. These were linked to an Inland Sector Operations Centre to process the incoming data and co-ordinate a response and the Gun Defended Areas to shoot down the aircraft as they approached. By the mid-1950s, all were obsolete. Jet aircraft flew higher and faster than the earlier piston-powered types, meaning the detection-to-response time was dramatically cut. Furthermore, the Royal Artillery could not reach the operating altitudes of the jets with anti-aircraft shells. The following four pictures illustrate the major components of the early air defence system.

Above left: RAF Bempton, East Yorkshire Coast. The concrete structures are designed to withstand air attack. Each carried a radar scanner when the station was operational.

Above right: RAF Kelvedon Hatch, Essex. This bungalow, intended to look like a farm worker's cottage, hides the entrance to a three-storey Sector Operations Centre bunker.

Right: AAOR Lansdown. This two-storey bunker on the outskirts of Bath was the final link in the early air defence chain. Operated by the Royal Artillery, this Anti-Aircraft Operations Room (AAOR) directed a number of gun batteries over Bristol defending the industrial centre and docks of the city.

By the 1970s, Air Defence had become a multi-layered network involving a wide range of weapon, detection and tracking systems. Essentially the air threat was the same; however, Soviet aircraft now carried an array of 'stand-off' weapons rather than bombs intended to be dropped over the target. This change in tactics dictated that British air defence should be able to intercept as many aircraft as possible as far away from her shores as possible. The following pictures serve to illustrate the sequence of events following the detection of an unidentified aircraft in the early 1980s. This situation was played out at least once or twice a week for the last two decades of the Cold War. Interestingly, Russia recommenced such missions in 2006.

Radar Type AN/FPS-6 HF. This shot illustrates how rudimentary early Cold War radar was. The AN/FPS-6 Height Finder was one of a multitude of scanners that were to be found on RAF stations in the first two decades after the Second World War.

Above: An Avro Shackleton on Airborne Early Warning patrol over the North Sea detects a suspect contact with its chin-mounted AN/APS-20 radar. The aircraft, from No. 8 Squadron based at RAF Lossiemouth, transmits the data to a Sector Operations Centre (SOC) at RAF Boulmer, Northumberland. They interrogate the information and ascertain the contact is not civilian. NATO is informed.

Right: The height finders (foreground) and tracking radar (behind) at RAF Staxton Wold, Yorkshire, confirm the contact as fast moving and at high altitude. The SOC now informs 11 Group of the incursion. (*Scarborough Evening News*)

English Electric Lightning interceptors, held on Quick Reaction Alert (QRA) at RAF Binbrook, are scrambled. The supersonic fighters are off the tarmac in ninety seconds, heading out over the east coast whilst climbing to 16,500+ metres. They are being controlled by the SOC via Staxton Wold. (Courtesy Ministry of Defence)

Two McDonnell Douglas Phantoms are scrambled from RAF Wattisham, East Anglia. They meet up with a KC-135 Stratotanker of the 306th Strategic Refuelling Wing, RAF Mildenhall, Suffolk, over the North Sea, for in-flight refuelling before heading out north to support the Lightnings. (Department of Defense Imagery photo no. DF-ST-82-04398)

Meanwhile the Lightnings have paid the price for reaching the search area so quickly. They rendezvous with a Handley Page Victor tanker from 57 Squadron, RAF Marham, Norfolk. Once tanked the interceptors are controlled by the Shackleton, acting as a forward air command, itself using data link from the SOC and onboard air warfare specialists.

The Lightnings intercept the target, identifying it as a Soviet TU-95 Bear G. The Bear is already an old aircraft but it is also a formidable weapons platform. The Bear G is capable of carrying the KH-22 missile, a nuclear-tipped weapon designed to destroy an entire US carrier fleet in one go. Later models were armed with KH-22 cruise missiles for use against strategic targets. In the UK, these could be ports, power stations or even towns and cities with industrial assets. (Department of Defense Imagery photo no. DN-SC-85-06031)

Above: The Lightnings move in to photograph the aircraft. The rear gunner keeps his twin barrels pointing up, a signal that there is no hostility towards the British fighters, even waving at the RAF pilots. The same cannot be said for the electronics officer in the observation portal. His message is clear! For twenty minutes, the aircraft continues its course towards the British mainland.

Left: NATO raises the threat level, activating the Bloodhound Mk II batteries based at RAF West Raynham, Norfolk. The SOC now filters information to the Fire Control Centre manning the missiles in case the Bear continues on its current course. The Bloodhound was a potent weapon if, by the 1980s, a little long in the tooth. Capable of intercepting an aircraft at 20,000+ metres at a distance of over 185 km, once the missile was within a preset distance of the target it detonated, shredding the aircraft with tungsten rods and shrapnel. (Department of Defense Imagery photo no. DF-ST-83-00493)

Above left: A number of short-range interceptors are also placed on high readiness. These aircraft are intended to meet the incoming enemy as they cross the North Sea and comprise a number of types including Hunters (seen here) and Hawks. In an emergency, anything with a weapons capability would be pressed into service.

Above right: Airfield defence now initiates in case an enemy aircraft gets through. RAF Regiment Rapier crews have deployed to designated points around the airfield and, through a mobile command unit and eight missile units, have around 500 sq.km covered. The Rapier was battle-proven in the Falklands and the crews are confident of its capabilities. They are stood down when the Soviet aircraft turns back towards the Motherland. (Courtesy BAe Systems)

Right: If the order had come to stop the aircraft, the Phantom interceptor would fire a Sparrow or Sky Flash (dependent on date) from a range of 40 km, where it would close on the target at speeds in excess of Mach 3. (Courtesy Ian Lewis)

NBC

During the Second World War, if an air raid was called, you could be pretty certain it would be something involving high explosives or incendiaries – unfortunately this was not the case in the Cold War. A major concern to the NATO forces from the 1960s was the possibility of chemical or biological warfare. All member nations were involved in the development of equipment to counter the threat; the infamous Porton Down on the edge of Salisbury Plain was responsible for the UK's effort. A Porton Down speciality was VX, an extremely effective nerve agent discovered by ICI. Whilst the Government publicly reported it was only developed for research, it secretly sold vast quantities to the United States. Contamination from nuclear fallout was also a very real possibility if war had started. British equipment was intended to stop the ingestion of dust. Only having thick solid protection by buildings or sheltering underground would effectively protect against radiation. Naturally, the local population would not be provided with personal protection at the outbreak of war. Various attempts to ban chemical and biological agents by binding agreement were politically supported but secret stockpiles were maintained by both sides.

Porton Down, Salisbury Plain. Situated on the southern edge of the Plain and surrounded by 8,000 acres of Wiltshire grassland, Porton Down was the focal point for all British chemical and biological weapon development. However, several sites around the United Kingdom were involved in research and production.

Decontamination is a complex business, especially where aircraft are concerned. Many front line bases had specifically designed 'wash down' stations that removed the majority of contaminants from the aircraft as it taxied past. These two pictures show Royal Air Force groundcrew in full NBC suits decontaminating a Phantom II during a simulated chemical attack at RAF Leeming. The RAF and USAF constantly trained together. These aircraft were from the Missouri Air National Guard, detached to Britain as part of Exercise Coronet Cactus in 1982. (Department of Defense Imagery photo nos. DF-ST-83-06939 & DF-ST-83-06940)

Not every defence procurement process had a successful outcome and when mistakes were made they were more often than not very expensive. What follows are a few of those projects that were under development during the Cold War but for one reason or another never made it past the prototype stage. As some of the following shots are publicity material we felt there was value in quoting the original information, if only to demonstrate the manufacturers' optimism.

Above: BIG BRUISER – This is Britain's new Caernarvon tank, described by the War Office as 'probably the most powerful tank in the world.' It will soon face exhaustive tests in Britain and overseas. It is claimed to have better armour and a more powerful engine than the Centurion, which won high praise from the Allies in Korea. Only twenty-one examples were built as the project was scrapped in favour of the more mobile Conqueror tank.

Left: British Aerospace Nimrod AEW Mk.3. The first Airborne Early Warning NIMROD AEW Mk.3 (XZ286) made its maiden flight from British Aerospace's Woodford Airfield on 16 July 1980 to begin the aircraft's development programme. After entering service in 1982 the aircraft will provide early warning coverage for the UK Air Defence Region, East Atlantic and the Channel, the NATO areas currently patrolled by Shackleton AEW aircraft. The project was cancelled in 1986 after £1 billion had been invested. The Shackleton continued on until 1991; by then it had given forty-two years of service.

Above: Tactical Strike and Reconnaissance aircraft – TSR2. Crewing in at A&AEE Boscombe Down. TSR2 was much more than a low-level, supersonic, nuclear bomber. It was the aircraft that the very future of the entire British aviation community relied on. To be eligible to bid for lucrative contracts, companies were forced to amalgamate, eventually forming the British Aircraft Corporation (BAC).

Right: Classified as a 'prestige' project, the returned Wilson Government chopped the TSR2 programme in April 1965. Quickly afterwards the aircraft were unceremoniously destroyed.

Germany and the NATO commitment

British armed forces had been involved in the protection of West Germany since its inception in 1949. Throughout the Cold War this presence formed part of the wider NATO remit to ensure no attack on Western Europe by Soviet, and later, Warsaw Pact, troops would be successful. The British Army on the Rhine (BAOR) was formed on 25 August 1945, primarily to control the British Zone of Occupation and Berlin Sector occupied at the end of the Second World War. By the 1970s, over 56,000 British troops were stationed in West Germany, including those armed with tactical nuclear weapons.

Above: Blue Streak Medium Range Ballistic Missile. Blue Streak was an ambitious plan to develop Britain's own silo-launched, ballistic missile. The project, initiated in 1955, pushed the technological boundaries of all the companies involved. By 1960, having cost £450 million and with no end in site, the missile was cancelled. The launcher went on to be used by the European Space Programme until 1970.

Right: Fairey Rotordyne. The Rotordyne first flew in November 1957 and was intended for military and civil applications. Government funding of around £5 million, a substantial sum, was promised. Unfortunately, orders from the RAF never materialised, nor did any from British European Airways, who had initially indicated there would be. By 1962, all funding had dried up and the Rotordyne was cancelled. (Photo: J Thinesen, SFF photo archive)

This page: Erecting a battlefield nuclear weapon in Northern Europe. The Corporal Battlefield Nuclear Weapon was operated by the Royal Artillery in West Germany between 1954–1964. It had an estimated range of around 130 km but was extremely unreliable, the British test fire success being less than 50 per cent, a product of its liquid-fuelled motor. It was replaced by 1964 by another battlefield nuke – Honest John. Other nuclear weapons included 'the atomic howitzer' and a nuclear mine capable of punching a huge gap in any advancing army.

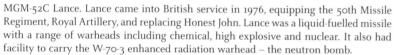

MGM-52C Lance. Lance came into British service in 1976, equipping the 50th Missile Regiment, Royal Artillery, and replacing Honest John. Lance was a liquid-fuelled missile with a range of warheads including chemical, high explosive and nuclear. It also had facility to carry the W-70-3 enhanced radiation warhead – the neutron bomb.

Above left: Missile being loaded at Pombsen, West Germany. (Courtesy of Andrew Law)

Above right: Inspection at Pombsen. (Courtesy of Andrew Law)

Right: Lance salvo at the White Sands Missile Range, United States in 1987. The weapons system was withdrawn from service in 1992. (Department of Defense Imagery photo no. DA-SC-88-01650)

Left and below: Bridge building. The ability to press forward into a wave of Warsaw Pact armour was central to all NATO planning. To ensure total mobility, the British Army were extremely proficient at bridge construction. Here, Ghurkhas construct a bridge for a Chieftain tank.

Above: Copehill Down, Salisbury Plain, was built in the mid-1980s to simulate a typical Eastern European town. (Courtesy of Ian Barnes)

Urban Combat. Not all fighting would be done on the sprawling plains of Central Europe. History had taught both sides that it would be in the towns and cities that the cost would be highest.

Above: Practising House Clearance at the Ruhleben training facility, West Germany, 1989. (Courtesy of Andrew Law)

Below left: A Chieftain tank, in disruptive camouflage, practicing restrictive manoeuvres at the Ruhleben training facility, West Germany 1989. (Courtesy of Andrew Law)

RAFG

The Royal Air Force operated in large numbers across West Germany throughout the 1950s, primarily as a legacy of the Second World War. From the 1960s, the remaining stations had a dual role. In peace time they operated as a national force protecting British interests but on transition to war they became part of the NATO air force under the banner 2 Allied Tactical Air Force. In that guise, the RAF worked alongside units from the USA, Belgium, West Germany and the Netherlands. A wide number of aircraft were operated throughout the Cold War but, by the early 1980s, this had been reduced to four specific types.

Above left: Jaguar HAS site, RAF Brüggen. The Sepecat Jaguar was a collaboration project between France and Britain and was intended to fill a requirement for an advanced jet trainer and tactical support aircraft. Throughout the 1970s and 1980s, a considerable number of Jaguars were stationed in Germany at RAF Brüggen and Laarbrüch. An extensive system of Hardened Aircraft Shelters (HAS) spread across Western Europe from the early 1970s in an attempt to protect aircraft from strafing fire or shrapnel during an attack.

Above right: Harrier. The Harrier was the only viable Vertical Take-off and Landing (VTOL) aircraft of the Cold War. The type proved itself during the Falklands campaign in both the fighter and ground attack roles. Predominantly stationed in Germany throughout the 1970s and 1980s, the aircraft were able to operate from improvised hides with little or no prior preparation. The aircraft were stationed at RAF Gütersloh, the most easterly of the British airbases. As a formidable ground attack and support aircraft, the Harrier would be expected to crush any armour crossing the border into West Germany.

Right: McDonnell Douglas Phantom. The Phantom assumed the interceptor role over the Lightning at all RAF Germany stations. By the early 1980s, this was Nos 19 and 92 Squadron at RAF Wildenrath. The aircraft carried Sparrow and Sidewinder air-to-air missiles and, in a centre-line pod, a 20 mm M61A1 Vulcan cannon. The type was steadily replaced by the Tornado through the late 1980s.

This page: Tornado delivering JP233 Runway Denial Weapon. The Panavia Tornado was a tri-national (UK, Italy, West Germany) project. The aircraft was capable of penetrating the Warsaw Pact air defences at extreme low level, partially aided by 'fly-by-wire' technology and a terrain-following radar, essentially at 50 m or less. By 1985, most of the West German RAF stations had converted from Jaguar and Phantom to the Tornado. Of the considerable conventional weapons loaded, by far the most violent (ignoring the nuclear aspects) was the JP233 runway denial weapon. JP233 was a centreline-mounted delivery system carrying thirty SG-357 runway-cratering sub-munitions and 215 HB-876 anti-personnel mines. Once deployed, the paved runway was rendered useless as the sequence here shows. (BAe Systems)

Anti-Submarine and Shipping

With Britain being an island nation and gateway to the North Atlantic, it came as no surprise that the RAF and RN should form a major part of NATO's anti-submarine and shipping patrols as well as defending the coastline and trade routes. From the late 1960s, this function became ever more critical as nuclear weapons were loaded into submarines.

Blackburn Buccaneer about to land on the *Ark Royal*. The Buccaneer entered service in 1962. In addition to conventional ordnance, including the Martel Anti-shipping missile, the Buccaneer was type-approved for the delivery of the Red Beard and later WE-177 nuclear devices. All nuclear stores were carried internally in the aircraft's rotating bomb-bay. Six Fleet Air Arm squadrons were equipped with the aircraft until the last true fixed-wing carrier, HMS *Ark Royal*, was decommissioned in 1978. The aircraft then passed to the RAF.

Nimrod: The Mighty Hunter. By the 1980s, 18 Group RAF had inherited the majority of the maritime activities the service performed; within the group were the Nimrod squadrons. Nimrod first flew in 1968 and continues to support maritime missions to this day. The large unpressurised pannier extending from the nose is the equipment bay. This allowed the aircraft to carry a formidable array of weaponry for the detection and destruction of enemy shipping and submarines.

Submarine Chasing. Flights across the Atlantic, Western Approaches and Mediterranean were commonplace in the hunt for Soviet submarines. Here, a French Daphné class submarine is 'buzzed' by a Nimrod. Naturally, the Russian crews were not so obliging, forcing the aircraft to stay aloft for ten hours or more at a time on search missions. (Courtesy Andy Stryker)

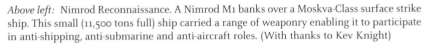

Above left: Nimrod Reconnaissance. A Nimrod M1 banks over a Moskva-Class surface strike ship. This small (11,500 tons full) ship carried a range of weaponry enabling it to participate in anti-shipping, anti-submarine and anti-aircraft roles. (With thanks to Kev Knight)

Above right: Kiev. Kiev was one of four 'heavy aviation cruisers' built by the Soviet administration between 1970–76. The ship layout was unusual: with an island and 2/3 angled-deck layout it was to all intents and purposes an aircraft carrier. However, the front third of the ship carried anti-shipping missile batteries. This configuration dictated that only VSTOL and helicopters could operate from the deck. Naturally, she was shadowed by NATO forces whenever possible.

Right: Minsk. Viewed from port, the Kiev-class carrier *Minsk* photographed during a low pass by a Lockheed Electra during a NATO exercise in 1982. Four VSTOL Yak-38 (NATO code Forger) can be clearly seen on the forward flight deck. Forger was developed for use in the anti-shipping and air-defence role specifically required by the Kiev-class ships, where VSTOL was essential. The aircraft was nowhere near as successful as the Harrier. For a start, it had three engines and in hot conditions the payload had to be radically down-sized to allow the aircraft to get off the deck! (Department of Defense Imagery photo no. DN-SN-83-01340)

Deterrent

Britain has been involved in the development of nuclear weapons since the 'Manhattan Project', culminating in the detonation on 16 July 1945 in New Mexico of *Trinity* – the first true nuclear weapon. That test led directly to the first and only offensive use of nuclear weapons in war through the destruction of Hiroshima and Nagasaki on 6 and 9 August that same year. Britain played a major part in the development of the second device via a mission led by William, later Lord, Penney. However, the United States Government had been unimpressed at the lack of British security, especially when a member of the mission, Alan Nunn May, was revealed as a major Russian spy in 1946, and cancelled any further collaboration. In 1947, the United Kingdom decided to build its own nuclear weapon and on 3 October 1952, at 09:30 local Monte Bello time, Britain stepped onto the nuclear stage. British weapons have never been placed on an aggressive footing, following instead the policy of deterrence. As the Government noted in 1983:

The essence of deterrence is that, to prevent war, or use of the threat of war, a country must itself maintain the instruments of war and make clear to any potential aggressor that it is willing to retaliate against aggression.

For a policy of deterrence to succeed military capabilities must be visible and credible. Weapons, both nuclear and conventional, must be modernised and effective; and there must be enough of them. But the purpose of maintaining these forces and these arsenals is that they should never need to be used and that peace is preserved.

The Policy of Deterrence. Defence and Disarmament Issues, October 1983, Arms Control and Disarmament Research Unit.

(NY8-Oct.23)FIRST OFFICIAL PICTURE OF BRITISH A-BOMB--This is the first official picture of the detonation of the British atom bomb at the Monte Bello Islands off the northwest Australian coast on Oct.3rd. This is an early stage of the explosion after the initial orange flash had been enveloped by the great uprush of water, clouds of steam, smoke and spray.(APWirephoto)(b51055BIS)1952 (See Wire Story,London dateline)

Hurricane. At 09:30 on 3 October 1952, Britain's first atomic device was detonated. The device had been contained in the depths of a redundant River Class frigate – HMS *Plym*. Time scales were tight to say the least. Production of weapons-grade plutonium had taken far longer than expected to produce. The reactors at Windscale, Cumbria, built specifically for the job, managed to fly out just enough material the day before the detonation.

Above: Blue Danube. By November 1953, the Royal Air Force had a nuclear capability through Blue Danube. The weapon was large and difficult to handle. At over 7.5m long and weighing over 4,500 kg, the RAF's largest bomber, the Valiant, only just managed to carry it, but this low yield (10–12 Kt) fission weapon still provided Britain with a truly independent deterrent.

Right: Grapple X. Britain conducted a number of atmospheric tests between 1957–58 at Christmas Island in the Pacific Ocean. On 8 November 1957, a Vickers Valiant piloted by Sqn Ldr B. Millet dropped the UK's first true thermonuclear device, achieving a yield of 1.8 megatons. By April 1958, a 3 megaton yield had been achieved. Now the United States began negotiations for a resumption of technical co-operation.

Thor Intermediate-Range Ballistic Missile (IRBM). Even with the successes of the Grapple tests, Britain was some way off developing an effective missile system. Adding to this was the slow production of the V force, not forecast to be fully operational until 1961 at the earliest. All this, coupled with the Soviets having a two-year lead on Intercontinental range missiles, forced the United States to ask for permission to locate IRBMs on British soil. The Government agreed as it plugged the British capability gap. Sixty missiles were stationed along the east coast of England between 1958 and late 1963.

Yellow Sun. The aptly-named Yellow Sun was Britain's first true thermonuclear weapon, developed from the Grapple programme. By 1959, the physics package, providing a yield of well over a megaton, was substantially smaller than the casing suggests. Yellow Sun was carried by the V-force until 1972. (Courtesy Royal Air Force Museum Hendon)

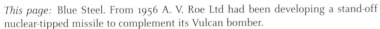

This page: Blue Steel. From 1956 A. V. Roe Ltd had been developing a stand-off nuclear-tipped missile to complement its Vulcan bomber.

Above left: On display at the 1960 Farnborough airshow.

Above right: Engine and instrumentation test facility at A&AEE Boscombe Down. A missile can be seen on the central gantry.

Right: Under slung on the Vulcan, Blue Steel would be released around 180 km from the target. It would climb to 21,000 m, cruise to the target then dive vertically into the centre with an accuracy of 160 m! (Courtesy of Adrian Balch collection)

Polaris. The problem with any airborne nuclear deterrent is it needs a runway to be effective. Likewise missiles, even in underground facilities, are vulnerable. Those launched from submarines are almost impossible to detect before launch. In 1969, the deterrent passed from the RAF to the Royal Navy in the form of the Resolution-Class nuclear-powered submarine carrying the Polaris Intercontinental Ballistic Missile (ICBM).

Above: Periscope shot of HMS *Resolution*. Note missile bay door open.

Left: A UGM-27 Polaris submarine-launched, ballistic missile is launched from HMS *Revenge* in 1986. (Department of Defense Imagery photo no. DF-SC-87-12795)

WE-177. WE-177 is Britain's longest-serving nuclear weapon. Three versions were in service between 1963 and 1998 with both the Royal Navy as a depth charge and the RAF as a free-fall bomb in both kiloton and megaton ranges. The performance of the WE-177 is still classified, but what *is* known is that even though the weapon is only a tenth of the size of Blue Danube, it had a thousand times the destructive power!

A test round for ascertaining the ballistic capabilities of the casing. This device is seen attached to a helicopter, suggesting that the weapon was to be used by the Royal Navy as a nuclear depth charge.

Chapter 4

AMERICANS

One of the most noticeable facets of the Cold War was the stationing of Super Power troops and weapons in friendly countries. The United States was welcomed by governments across Northern Europe, especially those who were members of the North Atlantic Treaty Organisation (NATO), from 1949. The Communist Bloc formed a similar organisation, the Warsaw Pact, when West Germany joined NATO in 1955. Neither side felt the need to directly confront the other, fighting by proxy instead, and thus an 'uneasy peace' was maintained across Europe. Consequently, the presence of the American military in Britain formed a major part of the Cold War story.

At the end of the Second World War the United States had indicated its intention to withdraw from Europe within two years. Indeed, by 1946, practically all stations used by the USAAF had reverted to the Royal Air Force and, in many cases, closure. The first hint of a reversal came in the summer of 1946. Whilst visiting airfields on the point of closure, Marshal of the Royal Air Force Lord Tedder and General Carl Spaatz, USAAF, discussed apparent Soviet belligerence on the Continent. Tedder, at Spaatz's request, agreed to upgrade five airfields – Marham, Lakenheath, Scampton, Bassingbourne and Mildenhall – making them capable of supporting long-range heavy bombers, namely the B-29. This period also saw the formation of two iconic American organisations: Strategic Air Command (21 March 1946) and the United States Air Force (16 September 1947). The airfield upgrades allowed Washington to threaten the Soviets with airpower when the Berlin Blockade quickly escalated from a border dispute into a full-scale siege. Just two years after the Spaatz-Tedder agreement, B-29s of the 28th and 307th Bomb Groups were in transit to their new bases. The first thirty aircraft of the 28th landed at RAF Scampton on 17 July 1948. Aircraft of the 307th Bomb Group took up residence at Marham and, a few weeks later, Lakenheath. By the end of August, ninety B-29s were in Britain on thirty-day temporary duty. This was steadily increased to sixty and then ninety days. The following extract from a Pentagon study in 1949 sums up the situation.

The United Kingdom has great strategic significance because of its manpower and industrial potential and its suitability as a base for air operations against the USSR. Loss of the United Kingdom would be a serious blow to Allied industrial capabilities, with a possible consequent increase in Soviet capabilities. These factors make the holding of the United Kingdom mandatory.

Operation Dropshot 1949.

The USAF is still in Britain sixty years later.

B-29. From 1948, USAF aircraft were to operate from stations across Britain, the B-29 flights being the first. The press quickly referred to them as the 'Atomic Bombers', helping hype up the threat to the Soviet administration. Nothing could have been further from the truth. It transpired that the United States did indeed possess nuclear weapons, two to be precise, both still in storage in America, but the precedent had been set.

Left: B-36. The B-36 re-affirmed the USAF global capacity. A massive six rear-facing piston engines, complemented by four jet engines, ensured the aircraft had a phenomenal range. Whilst never stationed in the UK, they were regular visitors between 1951–59. One aircraft crashed near Chippenham, Wiltshire, on 7 February 1953, whilst another landed short of the runway at RAF Boscombe Down. Amazingly it was towed onto the airfield with minimal damage.

Below left and right: Quick Reaction Alert (QRA). A B-45 'Tornado' crew on QRA at RAF Sculthorpe. By the 1950s, American aircrew, aircraft and atomic weapons – mostly hydrogen devices – were stationed in the United Kingdom. Crews and aircraft were kept at constant readiness, able to fly at the earliest opportunity, often airborne in fifteen minutes, deep into Soviet territory. This reaction time was radically curtailed with the development of intercontinental missile technology after Sputnik.

Above: B-47 Stratojet. The Stratojet was stationed at RAF Upper Heyford between 1952–65. Due to its poor range, it needed to be close to theatre to be effective, hence its association with Upper Heyford.

Right: F-101 Voodoo. The Voodoo was built in large numbers by the McDonnell Aircraft Corporation. In 1966, the 66th TRW and 17th and 18th TRSs relocated to RAF Upper Heyford, Bentwaters and Woodbridge from Laon AB, France, after the French government withdrew from NATO. This classic aircraft type was seen in the skies over southern England until 1970.

B-52. Arguably the most famous of all bomber aircraft, the B-52 has passed through Britain on a number of occasions but it has never been permanently stationed in the UK. This example was photographed on a visit to RAF Boscombe Down. The aircraft type replaced the B-36 in 1956 and continues to operate as the USAF's conventional bombing platform with a likely life up to 2035. (Courtesy of Pete James)

F-111. The General Dynamics F-111 was stationed in the United Kingdom from 1970, predominantly at RAF Upper Heyford and RAF Lakenheath. The aircraft took part in Operation *El Dorado Canyon* against Libya in 1986. The F-111 was the USAF's principal long-range, day and night interdiction fighter. It was capable of carrying two nuclear weapons in the internal bomb bay as well as a range of conventional ordnance. This shot shows aircraft flown by the 20th Tactical Fighter Wing over their home station of RAF Upper Heyford. (Photographer TSGT Jose Lopez: Department of Defense Imagery photo no. DF-ST-83-11409)

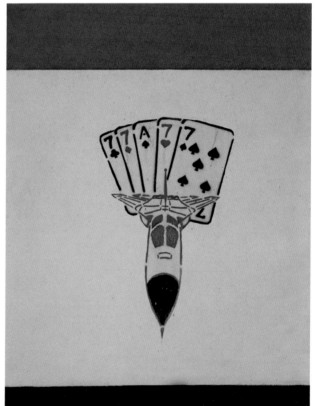

Above left: A-10 Thunderbolt (Warthog). A-10s first appeared in Britain in 1979, operating from RAF Woodbridge and its close neighbour RAF Bentwaters. Basically a gun platform, the aircraft had a devastating fire capability in the close battlefield support role. The primary weapon is the GAU-8 Avenger Gatling Gun, delivering a possible 4,200 30 mm rounds per minute. The 81st TFW of RAF Bentwaters/RAF Woodbridge operated rotating detachments of A-10s at four bases in Germany known as Forward Operating Locations (FOLs): Leipheim, Sembach Air Base, Nörvenich, and Ahlhorn. If Warsaw Pact tanks had rolled over the border, the A-10 would have quite literally stopped them in their tracks.

Above right: GAU-8 Avenger Gun. What lies beneath. The A-10 Thunderbolt was designed with this gun in mind. In this USAF publicity shot, the GAU-8 is compared with a VW Beetle for scale. It was not to truly demonstrate its awesome firepower until the first Gulf War where the gun consigned over 4,500 tanks, vehicles and artillery pieces to the scrap heap.

Below right: 77th Tactical Fighter Squadron hangar art.

Above: An air-to-air view of an RF-4 Phantom II aircraft flown by the 10th Tactical Reconnaissance Wing, flanked by two F-5 Tiger II aircraft flown by the 527th Tactical Fighter Training Squadron, known as the Aggressors. The Aggressors acted as the enemy in all tactical or operation scenarios. The 527th were originally stationed at RAF Alconbury but, towards the end of the Cold War, had moved to RAF Bentwaters. (Department of Defense Imagery photo no. DF-ST-84-05831)

Left: From 1979, RAF Fairford was the home of the 11th Strategic Group operating the KC-135 Stratotanker, known as the European tanker force. The aircraft were capable of refuelling practically any USAF aircraft and regularly serviced reconnaissance flights such as this one by an RF-4C of 26th Tactical Reconnaissance Wing, Zweibrücken, West Germany. The tanker was a familiar sight in the skies above Gloucestershire. (Courtesy Ian Lewis)

Opposite left: Staff Sergeant (SSGT) John Reynolds, left, and Sergeant (SGT) Dennis Birch of the 501st Tactical Missile Wing use a Mark-97 test set while performing maintenance on a GLCM transporter-erector-launcher. (Department of Defense Imagery photo no. DF-ST-85-05266)

Opposite right: GLCM Alert and Maintenance Area (GAMA). A series of bomb-proof shelters were built at both RAF Greenham Common and RAF Molesworth, each in a segregated compound. Each shelter housed two mobile Launch Control Centres (LCC) and four Transporter Erector Launchers (TEL), one set being held at immediate readiness. The shelters were designed to withstand conventional attack and, hopefully, an airburst above the station.

Cruise

No account of Britain's Cold War would be complete without a mention of one of the most controversial aspects of the United States European deployment. At the centre of this are RAF Greenham Common, Margaret Thatcher and the Conservative Government and, of course, the Peace Camps. The decision to modernise nuclear forces deployed in the European Theatre was taken on 12 December 1979. The Soviets had spent the year deploying SS-20 mobile-launched missile systems and in so doing demonstrated that NATO was woefully under-resourced. The answer was to deploy mobile Pershing II missiles on the Continent and Tomahawk Ground Launched Cruise Missile (GLCM) wings in a further six locations, ninety-six at RAF Greenham Common and a further sixty-four at RAF Molesworth. The military aspects of these deployments are shown here; the women's camp can be found in 'The Public' chapter.

Above left: Airman First Class Greg (A1C) A. Fournier, a member of the 501st Tactical Missile Wing, drives a 10-ton tractor-trailer as it pulls a transporter-erector-launcher for GLCMs. The launchers would disperse into the English countryside if conflict broke out. On peacetime manoeuvres, CND and others made sure this was anything other than easy. (Department of Defense Imagery photo no. DF-ST-85-05262)

Above right: Control Centre, RAF Greenham Common. This building performed a number of functions. Made to look like an office block, a substantially protected site was concealed within it, visible at the right hand of the building. It controlled the defence of the airfield, primarily the GAMA site and when and where the LCCs and TELs were deployed. It could withstand conventional, chemical and low-yield nuclear attack.

Right: Bomb Dump Igloos. This type of bomb storage facility was universally accepted in 1950 and examples can be found across NATO countries. They comfortably accommodated the largest of the hydrogen bombs, the Mk 17, that Strategic Air Command operated.

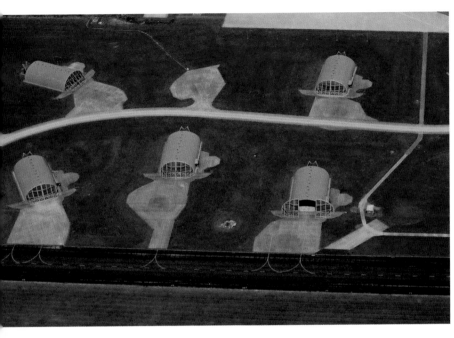

Above: Hardened Aircraft Shelters, RAF Boscombe Down. Part of the Co-located Operating Base (COB) network, this site would, on transition to war, accept two squadrons of F-111s. These could be relocated from existing UK-based assets or on deployment from the United States.

Right: Ammunition Store, RAF Welford. To supplement the already vast stockpile of ammunition held on specific RAF stations, Strategic Air Command took control of RAF Welford, West Berkshire, on 1 September 1955. The depot then supplied conventional weapons to all USAF stations in the United Kingdom; special weapons were held at squadron airfields.

Home From Home

Above left: The Commissary. A series of mall-sized commissaries were built across RAF stations playing host to US service personnel. The idea was to sell familiar goods and produce to service families who were stationed abroad and in so doing make them feel less isolated. To give some idea of the scale of the operation, the commissary service took $2.1 billion in 1986, making it the twelfth largest food-retailer in America. (Photographer Sgt Olan A. Owens. Department of Defense Imagery photo no. DF-ST-83-04651)

Above right: 'Tobacco Housing'. In the mid-1950s it was recognised that American servicemen were likely to be stationed for long periods in the United Kingdom. The old wartime Nissen huts were clearly inadequate and, subsequently, the British Government built a series of married quarters at a number of stations. They were paid in American tobacco. Officially known as surplus commodity housing, they locally became known as 'tobacco houses'.

Left: Instantly recognisable as a piece of United States street furniture, the fire hydrant can also be found on any RAF station seconded to the USAF. Put simply, the fire appliances used on site were always shipped from the USA and could not connect to the standard British main. They also helped give the impression of a home from home for service families.

Chapter 5

SPIES AND INTELLIGENCE GATHERING

The ability to warn against impending attack, the development of new weapons or the subversion of the governmental system in a target country became a fundamental part of the Cold War. Often portrayed as a shadowy world, so typified by the work of Ian Fleming or John le Carré, both East and West went to extraordinary lengths to discover what the other side was doing. Some operations were purely military, intended to give information of troop movements or equipment parks close to the border between NATO and the Warsaw Pact. Others took a more subtle approach like Operation *Scrum Half*, a joint UK-US initiative to deny Soviet-influenced countries imported consumer goods, but on both sides were the spies.

The reasons for espionage or the betrayal of one's country are often difficult to ascertain. Some carried out their dark work in an attempt to make a better world in which all sides were the same, others were blackmailed – often after some dubious sexual liaison – and some just enjoyed the thrill of the chase. Whatever the reasons, people died because of their actions and not in usual 'James Bond fashion'. Julius and Ethel Rosenberg died in the electric chair in 1953 in the USA whilst Dmitri Fyodorovich Polyakov, a Soviet general passing information to the CIA, was executed with a single bullet to the back of the neck in March 1988. Polyakov was betrayed by Aldrich Hazen Ames, a CIA operative under the employ of the KGB, who is currently serving a life sentence for his part in the 'disappearance' of several CIA operatives across eastern Europe.

The U2 was first introduced in 1956 after an incredible eighteen-month development. The CIA operated the aircraft, capable of reaching 21,000+ metres, regularly overflying the Soviet Union from bases in Pakistan and Turkey, photographing missile sites and airfields. In May 1960, one was shot down over the USSR whilst another succumbed to ground fire whilst photographing areas of Cuba in October 1962. From 1983, a Tactical Reconnaissance version of the aircraft regularly operated out of RAF Alconbury. (Department of Defense Imagery photo no. DF-SC-83-10874)

Opposite left: RAF Chicksands, Bedfordshire. The station passed to the United States Air Force in early 1960 and, in 1963, a circular array known locally as 'the elephant cage' was built. A similar structure was to appear at RAF Blakehill Farm some two years later. The AN/FLR-9 antenna performed two functions, relaying secure communications across Europe whilst also intercepting signals traffic from the east.

Opposite right: Bakan, North Sea. Throughout the Cold War every opportunity was taken to gather information on the other side's activities. One lucrative, if rather obvious, method was to disguise your intent with something more mundane. The Soviet navy built a fleet of trawlers for intelligence operations. By the 1970s, a large number of suspicious vessels had been recorded by the RAF and Royal Navy, especially during NATO exercises. British intelligence was much more discreet. They trained civilian trawler crews in recognition, armed them with cameras and paid for any photographs brought back.

Opposite bottom: SR-71 Blackbird. The first of the Lockheed Blackbirds were delivered to the CIA in 1962. Two years later, an uprated version was delivered to the USAF. Capable of Mach 3 and an operational height of 25,000+ metres, the aircraft was capable of giving detailed reconnaissance over 259,000 sq. km. The aircraft were stationed at RAF Mildenhall from 1976. (Department of Defense Imagery photo no. DF-ST-83-10618)

General Dynamics EF-111 Raven. Twelve Ravens, forming the 42nd Electronic Countermeasures Squadron, arrived at RAF Upper Heyford on 3 February 1984 and were stationed at the Oxfordshire base until the end of the Cold War. The aircraft jammed enemy airspace control, allowing F-111 bombers a clear run onto the target. They successfully blanketed Libyan air defence during Operation *El Dorado Canyon* in 1986. (Department of Defense Imagery photo no. DF-ST-87-13482)

RAF Upper Heyford Reconnaissance Centre. To support reconnaissance operations across Europe, a large interpretation centre was built at Upper Heyford. Mission information, coupled with satellite intelligence, was processed here before being passed out to the bomber squadrons and NATO. The centre also serviced avionic equipment for the EF-111. A similar structure was built at RAF Lakenheath. Both were intended to withstand blast and chemical attack.

Above: Klaus Fuchs, spy. Fuchs was a German refugee and theoretical physicist who was part of the British mission to Los Alamos during the Manhattan Project. He was exposed as a Soviet spy in January 1950 and sentenced to fourteen years in prison for his part in passing nuclear secrets to the East. It is estimated that Fuchs' treachery allowed the Soviet Union to acquire nuclear weapons at least two years ahead of estimates.

Right: Harold 'Kim' Philby, spy, codename 'Stanley'. Philby, a member of British intelligence since 1940, was also a committed socialist and NKVD, later KGB, operative. He passed secrets to the Soviet Union until his discovery in 1963.

Above The Berlin Tunnel, Berlin. Operation *Stopwatch* was a joint operation between the SIS (MI6) and the CIA to tap into landline communication from Soviet Army headquarters in Berlin. It necessitated a 450 m tunnel being dug from the American to the Soviet sector of the city. One of those at the initial meeting was George Blake, a Soviet spy, who immediately let the KGB know of the plan. The KGB allowed the tunnel to go ahead and fed it misleading information for eleven months before 'discovering' it in April 1956. Only ten years later did the West discover the tunnel had been compromised and that some, if not all, the hard-won intelligence was suspect.

Left: Anthony Blunt, spy, codename 'Johnson'. Blunt passed information to the Soviet Union throughout the Second World War and in its immediate aftermath. When Guy Burgess and Donald Maclean defected to Moscow in May 1951, Blunt came under suspicion. He was interrogated by MI5 throughout 1952 but convinced them he was not an agent. In 1979 he was finally exposed.

Above left: Audley Square, London. 'On the right hand side of this little square is a prominent lamp post. A white figure '8' is painted at the base of the lamp post on the road side, about a metre from the pavement. I would put a light blue chalk mark below the figure '8' which would mean I was filling the DLB [Dead Letter Box] the same day'. Extract from page 60, 'Comrade Kryuchkov's instructions: top secret files on KGB foreign operations, 1975–85'.

Above right: Cultural Exchange. The idea of a cultural exchange often gave the opportunity for information gathering. When the Soviet Army Ensemble visited London in 1956, a number of the officers were KGB. Others took the opportunity to defect, Rudolph Nureyev in 1961 whilst performing in Paris and ballerina Natalia Makarova to England in 1970. Bulgarian dissident writer Georgi Markov was later murdered in London using the poisoned tip of an umbrella in 1978.

Above and right: Government Communications Headquarters (GCHQ) warnings about secrets and spies.

Left: East German Border Guard, 1979. Observation of the West was never covert at the Iron Curtain. The border between the GDR and FRG was constantly patrolled by both sides. However, it was the East that was obsessed with the documentation of every event and not just on the border. Life in the DDR became ever more restrictive as the Ministry for State Security, the Stasi, recorded all facets of everyday life. It rightfully gained the reputation as one of the most repressive organisations in the Communist world. Little wonder then that people were willing to risk their lives to flee to the West. (Department of Defense Imagery photo no. DA-ST-86-06122)

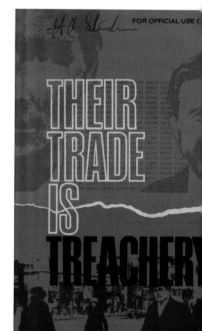

Oakley, Cheltenham. Britain's primary intelligence service throughout the Cold War was GCHQ, formed in 1946. The service relocated to two sites in Cheltenham between 1950–52 and in 1954 'C' Block was built at the Oakley site, capable of housing at least 800 staff. The CIA and other NATO partnership countries had offices at the site.

Oakley, Cheltenham. Security was tight on the way into the site and even tighter on the way out. Anyone was liable to be stopped and their vehicle searched.

EXIT SEARCH PROCEDURES
ALL PERSONNEL ARE REMINDED THAT THEY ARE REQUIRED TO MAKE THE CONTENTS OF THEIR VEHICLE, HAND-LUGGAGE, ETC. AVAILABLE FOR INSPECTION WHEN REQUESTED TO DO SO.

Blakehill Farm, Wiltshire. GCHQ took over a number of sites from 1964, including the old Admiralty signals station at Irton Moor, Scarborough, and the airfield at Blakehill Farm, North Wiltshire. A number of experiments were conducted at Blakehill Farm including Over the Horizon Radar and transmission interception via an array similar to the AN/FPR-9 located at RAF Chicksands.

MI6, Vauxhall. Towards the end of the Cold War, the Secret Intelligence Service, known in the business as 'Box 850', after its old PO Box number, was rehoused in a purpose-built HQ in the centre of London. The move raised a number of items; firstly the Government finally admitted to the existence of MI6, their activities also became statute and, as a result, operatives now have to remain within the law.

Chapter 6

THE FOUR MINUTE WARNING

One phrase more than any other epitomises the Cold War in the eyes of the British Public – 'Four Minute Warning'. Indeed, it became part of popular culture and has defined the latter decades of the twentieth century. In this chapter we discover the public face of the 'Four Minute Warning' and the military need for it.

The Royal Observer Corps (ROC) was a voluntary organisation with a long, proven and effective history. Throughout the Second World War, it had been the 'eyes of Fighter Command', tracking, via plotting posts around the country, the direction, heading, height and speed of enemy bomber formations. However, four days after the surrender of Germany and the end of the war in Europe the ROC was stood down.

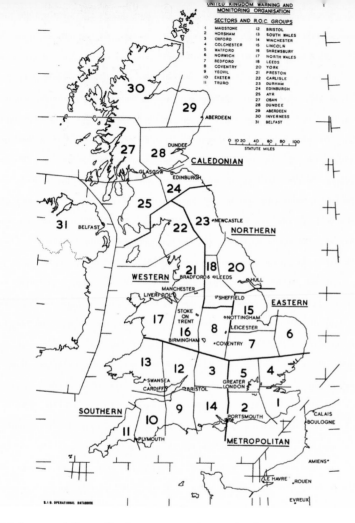

Above: Orlit Post. The stand-down was not to be a permanent arrangement and on 1 April 1947 the ROC was back in business. By 1952, a series of new posts were built around the country in an attempt to provide the ROC with standardised equipment. 413 'Orlit Posts' were constructed, each manned by a crew of three; tracking and aircraft identification remained the primary task at this time. Observers removed the lid to reveal rudimentary instrumentation.

Below: 20 Group Headquarters, York. Information from the posts around the country was telephoned into the appropriate Group HQ, which was in turn linked to one of six Fighter Command sectors. The information passed from the posts was plotted on a large, long-range map in the centre of the structure and Fighter Command was kept up to date with the developing situation, judging when and where to put up squadrons of Meteors as air defence.

ROC Sector and Group distribution, 1968. The British Isles were originally laid out like this for the aircraft reporting role, each sector aligned with Fighter Command and named by location. When the ROC took on the nuclear reporting role from the mid-1950s the national layout was retained, prevailing almost unchanged until 1991.

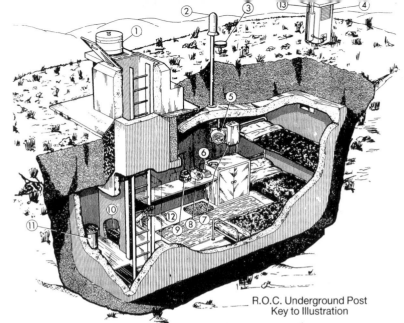

R.O.C. Underground Post
Key to Illustration

1. Ground Zero Indicator
2. Survey Meter Sensing Head
3. Bomb Power Indicator Sensing Head
4. Air Vent
5. Bomb Power Indicator
6. Fixed Survey Meter
7. Stand-By Radio Set
8. Tele-talk Set
9. Carrier Receiver
10. 12 Volt Battery
11. Chemical Closet
12. Pump for Pneumatic Aerial
13. Pneumatic Aerial

Above left: Underground Monitoring Post, Amesbury. In 1954, the Home Office decided that the ROC observation role was no longer a relevant proposition. Aircraft, powered by jet rather than piston, were flying faster and higher than ever before and now they were more likely to carry the far more devastating H-Bomb. And with the H-Bomb came the realisation that fallout would be a major debilitating factor of any nuclear exchange. The ROC found a new role in fallout and radiation monitoring; to protect from the effects of radiation the Corps was redeployed underground.

Above right: Underground Monitoring Post. The first of 1,563 posts was constructed in 1957. The programme was to continue for over ten years.

Above: Ballistic Missile Early Warning System, RAF Fylingdales, North Yorkshire. Of all the notable images from the Cold War the 'Golf Balls' at Fylingdales were, without doubt, the most recognisable symbols of the nuclear threat to Britain. Taking three years to build, the station was commissioned on 17 September 1963. The UKWMO was among the many recipients of information generated here. (Courtesy *Scarborough Evening News*)

Left: 20 Group Headquarters, York. In 1961, 20 Group was provided with a new HQ in keeping with the underground monitoring posts. Designed to operate under emergency conditions for thirty days, the building was semi-sunken to provide enhanced protection factor against radiation. A crew of up to sixty, including ROC personnel, scientific, Home Office and weather experts, operated the HQ at any one time. With this new task came a new task master – the United Kingdom Warning and Monitoring Organisation or UKWMO.

Above left: AWDREY. Each group HQ was fitted with a number of specialist recording devices, operational twenty-four hours a day. One such device was the Atomic Weapon Detection Recognition and Estimation of Yield – AWDREY for short. AWDREY was insurance against an 'out of the blue' attack. Using photoelectric cells, it was capable of recording the power of a detonation: useful for both fallout prediction and 'like for like' retaliation, a major role for the ROC.

Above right: Underneath each 'Golf Ball' was a single 25 m parabolic scanner, 10 m high and weighing a massive 112 tonnes. The AN/FPS-49 radar was capable of spotting an object 4,500 km distant so the moment one appeared above the horizon it was tracked. This would start the on-site calculation sequence and the clock running. (Courtesy *Scarborough Evening News*)

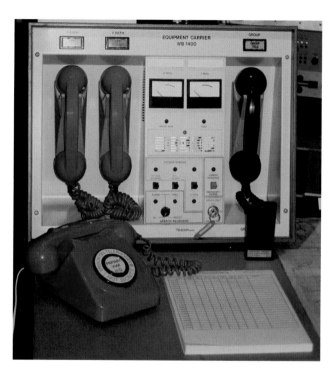

Above left: Threat Report. As an object was tracked by the massive radar arrays, speed, height and inclination were all fed into an impact predictor. The predictor then calculated the impact area using a number of preset scenarios including type of weapon and apogee. This was then fed to the Threat Report Board in the operations room, whereupon the senior officer would pass the information to the Home Office. Note the reading on the centre right 'mins-to-impact 03.5'. This is the origin of the 'Four Minute Warning'.

Above right: Warning District Headquarters, Swindon police station. Home Office representatives, based at the UK Regional Air Operations Centre, High Wycombe, would assess the threat before initiating a national warning. Britain was divided into 250 warning districts, each with a Carrier Control Point (CCP). On the turn of a single key, all 250 warning districts were activated simultaneously. At the same time the BBC would broadcast a pre-recorded 'Air Attack Red' message on all radio and television frequencies. Warning District HQs were housed in police or fire stations where possible. Swindon police station was built with a War Room in the basement and has small windows in the main block in an attempt to minimise blast damage.

Right: Carrier Control Point. A Carrier Control Point (CCP) was located in each War Room and it would be here that the local authorities would learn of the imminent attack. Through the red phones the operating officer would give the 'Attack Warning Red' signal and, by turning the key, would set off all the air-raid sirens in the warning district.

Above : Carrier Warning Point (CWP). A further device was used to warn those who lived in the country or outlying areas. The WB1400 was located in post offices, pubs and even private houses. On receiving the warning the recipient would warn others in the village by way of a hand-cranked siren, whistle, gong or maroon.

Left: Powered Siren. All major population areas in Britain had a number of powered sirens located within it. These were often on public buildings such as schools or fire stations; 7,000 were available by the mid-1970s. These were the only method of warning the general population of an imminent attack, maybe allowing some to take cover.

Rawlins Garage, Avebury. The CWP for the Avebury area was located at this local business. On receiving the warning, the local policeman was to cycle around the village giving the warning. By this point it would probably be too late to take cover.

Once the initial blast had passed, observers out on the monitoring posts collected readings and transmitted them back to Group HQ. *Right*: Here, an observer is collecting the data from the Ground Zero Indicator, a type of pin-hole camera that indicated the height and direction of the initial explosion. Once this was triangulated with other posts the centre point of the nuclear blast could be calculated. *Far right*: A close up image of the GZI device. The grey curving strip is caused by the passage of the sun.

Above: No. 14 Group Winchester. Duty Controller Observer Lt L. Tipping and Warning Officer Mrs M. Caldwell assessing fallout information being plotted by W/Observer R. Butler. Information directed in from the monitoring posts would be used to build a fallout picture. (Image No. P916(A) via Royal Observer Corps Museum)

Above right: Fallout Plotting. Ground Zero was indicated on the plotting board by a small mushroom cloud symbol with red for a ground burst, as this would produce the most fallout. Once the wind direction was taken into consideration, the path of the fallout could be predicted. In the bottom right-hand corner of this picture you can see a ground burst over Andover and the subsequent direction of the radioactive plume. The central black mushroom is an airburst over the airfield at RAF Upavon and the small red dots numbered in white show the locations of the underground monitoring posts.

Right: No. 2 Group, Horsham. Sector Control with International Liaison Desk in foreground. Other member nations of NATO often had a representative at Group HQs as fallout was no respecter of international boundaries. Once the footprint of the plume has been calculated a Fallout Warning Black is issued. Sirens run in populated areas and out on the posts a hand-cranked siren or maroons fire off three loud bangs. It is at this point that those who have followed the instructions of *Protect and Survive* hope it is enough! (Image No. P177(c) (MOD OS12 Neg 5797/31) via Royal Observer Corps Museum)

Chapter 7

BUNKER

One structure above all others typifies the British public's view of the Cold War: the so-called 'Nuclear Bunker', considered by many to be no more than a Government 'bolt hole' where hand-picked officials, Royalty and Ministers would hide, possibly for months, whilst the rest of the population was exposed to the full force of nuclear war. However, very few were built to withstand the effects of a direct nuclear strike and some were no more than council office basements. Changes in Government policy also drove many changes in protected site usage, leading to a confused network of regional, sub-regional and local controls. So where would Ministers and MPs, Councillors and other civil 'officials' go during a National Emergency? And rather more worrying, what was their remit once they were down there?

Home Defence Regions and Emergency Government

The idea of the Government protecting itself from harm was not specific to the Cold War: it had been around since the mid-1920s. The then Baldwin Government divided the United Kingdom into twelve Home Defence Regions (HDRs), each with a regional commissioner at its centre. The commissioner's remit was to co-ordinate the civil defence effort following an attack, probably from the air. By the outbreak of the Second World War, this had been expanded to include full state powers if Central Government was cut off. In the late 1940s, as the true nature of the threat from the east unfolded, the British Government re-adopted the HDR network. All subsequent planning for the protection of initially the population but, by the late 1960s, just the machinery of Government throughout the Cold War followed this layout. Many factors drove the types of bunkers that were constructed in support of Government including jet-engined aircraft and the speeds involved, the awesome destructive power of the hydrogen bomb over its smaller A-bomb predecessor, which political party was in power, and even how the Americans and Soviets conducted themselves in the United Nations.

Emergency Central Government Seat, Turnstile

Box Hill, near Corsham, Wiltshire, formerly a stone quarry and then an aircraft engine factory, was earmarked in the early 1950s as the seat of Emergency Central Government. By 1957, plans had been drawn up for a centre capable of coping with 7,000 government officials and support staff. Passenger and goods lifts were installed in 1957–1958, as was a new ventilation system and, rather bizarrely, a bar known as 'The Rose and Crown'. The Emergency Government Headquarters (EGHQ) could be accessed via the lifts, escalators or Box railway tunnel. The site was upgraded on a number of occasions and this included the amount of staff earmarked to use it. The site was placed in 'care and maintenance' in the late 1980s as three new super bunkers were nearing completion.

The Home Defence Regions. *'In any future war, central government would continue to function from its normal locations for as long as possible. Nevertheless, in a period of international tension or conventional attack, communications between London and the rest of the country could become overloaded or, later, disrupted. Therefore the United Kingdom has been divided into eleven regions. Regional Emergency committees would act as focal points for the co-ordination of essential services in each of these eleven regions under central government direction'.* (Civil Protection, Community Adviser Training Course, 1986)

HOME DEFENCE REGIONS

| REGION BOUNDARY | COUNTY BOUNDARY |
| ZONE BOUNDARY | METROPOLITAN COUNTY BOUNDARY |

Passenger Lift PL1, Turnstile. Underneath this mound is one access way to the vast Government Bunker at Box Hill. This structure alone was bigger than most local authority shelters. Civil servants and ministers who had been bussed from London would have used this facility to retreat to relative safety. (© Crown Copyright. Press release series by MOD DLO/DPA photography and Video Dept., Foxhill, Bath)

The eastern rail entrance to the facility was via the small square entrance, dwarfed by the much larger Box Tunnel to its left. (© Crown Copyright. Press release series by MOD DLO/DPA photography and Video Dept., Foxhill, Bath)

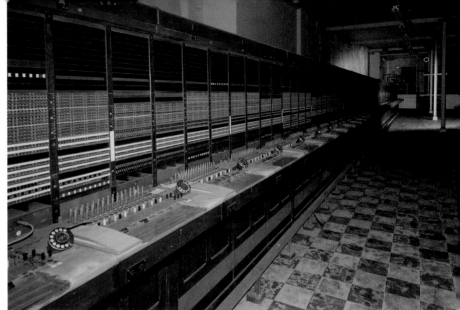

Above: Telephone Exchange, Turnstile. Communication with the outside world was essential if the Government was to maintain control post-attack. These units show equipment fitted in the early 1960s as part of a NATO-funded Emergency Manual Switching Scheme (EMSS). The EMSS provided secure trunking through a number of protected exchanges and allowed Turnstile to be in contact with every level of authority bunker around the UK. Had nuclear war broken out, these antiquated pieces of equipment would have looked decidedly modern. (© Crown Copyright. Press release series by MOD DLO/DPA photography and Video Dept., Foxhill, Bath)

Left: Escalator, Turnstile. This escalator, taken from the underground station at Holborn, would have helped the steady flow of officials descend to their protected offices. (© Crown Copyright. Press release series by MOD DLO/DPA photography and Video Dept., Foxhill, Bath)

Canteen, Turnstile. Whilst the rest of the population wondered if they had collected enough tins for fourteen days' food, the residents of Turnstile could expect a proper cooked meal. Here we see the ovens and servery from the canteen as refurbished in the early 1980s. (© Crown Copyright. Press release series by MOD DLO/DPA photography and Video Dept., Foxhill, Bath)

Laundry, Turnstile. Industrial-sized laundry facilities ensured all occupants of the Turnstile site would have clean clothes and sheets for the duration of their stay. (© Crown Copyright. Press release series by MOD DLO/DPA photography and Video Dept., Foxhill, Bath)

Prime Minister's bathroom, Turnstile. Whilst the fittings may seem a little antiquated, remember that, in the event of a nuclear attack, large parts of the country would have little chance of experiencing these basic necessities. (© Crown Copyright. Press release series by MOD DLO/DPA photography and Video Dept., Foxhill, Bath)

Broadcast Station, Turnstile. The facility at Box was vast – some estimates put it at over 400,000 sq. m – so an internal broadcast system was used to disseminate orders and information. It conjures up visions of a bizarre holiday camp atmosphere from the 1950s. (© Crown Copyright. Press release series by MOD DLO/DPA photography and Video Dept., Foxhill, Bath)

Coffee Maker, Turnstile. One function of Turnstile was to provide an alternative site for ordering nuclear retaliation. Facilities such as these would be a prerequisite. (© Crown Copyright. Press release series by MOD DLO/DPA photography and Video Dept., Foxhill, Bath)

Above left: Decay in Turnstile. One problem with subterranean life is the location of the water table. Turnstile is partially connected to Spring Quarry and, as the name implies, moisture is an ever-present problem, especially with electronic communications equipment. This image depicts more than just decay, it also symbolises the diminishing role the government would play in civil life, post-Armageddon. (© Crown Copyright. Press release series by MOD DLO/DPA photography and Video Dept., Foxhill, Bath)

Above right: Chilmark Regional Government Headquarters. Chilmark was one of three new structures commissioned in the mid-1980s to supersede the Turnstile site, dispersing central government to each, therefore making it more difficult to sever the head of the nation's defences. With room for 200+ civil servants, this vast structure was only operational for four years. It was equipped with everything from a full canteen to fitted carpets.

Regional Seats of Government

Of course, the United Kingdom could not be controlled from one central unit and so each HDR was divided into two administrative areas. These can be recognised on the HDR map in this section by the large singular number signifying the region followed by the .1 or .2 sub-division. Each sub-division contained a protected site known as a Sub-Regional Control (S-RC), headed by a junior minister. The function of the S-RC is best described in the following extract:

Sub-Regional Headquarters would be set up before attack in premises designed for minimum vulnerability and equipped with special communications. They would have no pre-attack executive function, but would operate immediately an attack took place which terminated normal central government.

The Machinery of Government in War, Home Defence College paper NRW/ MJW 751013

The minister in charge (Regional Commissioner) had as support staff representatives from the armed forces, fire service, police and utilities including water, electricity and gas. Members of the voluntary services including Red Cross and Women's Voluntary Service as well as the main ministries (Home Office, Ministry of Agriculture, Fisheries and Food, Central Office of Information, etc.) would also secure a 'seat' on this emergency administration. It is at this level of protected site that we encounter the inventiveness of, initially, the Home Office but, by the 1980s, also the Cabinet. The following examples serve to demonstrate that.

S-RC 8.2, Brackla, South Wales. Originally part of a Royal Ordnance Factory, the Home Office refurbished two magazines to protection standard in the early 1960s. The primary unit comprises an 80 m double-decked control capable of a four-week isolation period. The unit was mirrored exactly in the next magazine and the two were joined by a concrete tunnel running from the back corner of the primary to the front of the second. Estimations of staffing have ranged from 2 to 600. One thing is clear: not a mile from the site is a substantial Territorial Army barracks, suggesting the general public would not be amongst the lucky few to gain a seat.

Opposite: S-RC 4.2 (later 5.1), Kelvedon Hatch, Essex. Kelvedon Hatch, a former Rotor-period R4 Sector Operations Centre, was converted to a S-RC in 1961. Entrance to the three-storey bunker was disguised by this bungalow, intended to look like a farm labourer's cottage. Continued communications with other bunkers in the network and Central Government was paramount to the whole ethos of maintaining the machinery of Government, necessitating a large amount of equipment dedicated to that purpose. This in turn required a large staff, 200 to be precise, to maintain it as well as many high-ranking civil servants interested in the survival of the 'system'; for them sleeping arrangements would be cramped. (courtesy of J.A. Parrish & Sons)

The County Council in War

Below the various tiers of Government came the Local Authority and its responsibilities during times of crisis. The County Council's role was best described as:

In time of war the Chief Executive would become the County Controller responsible to and under the direction of the Regional Commissioner. He would be assisted by a small emergency committee comprising elected members who would be consulted on matters relating to the disposition of council resources essential to the life of the community. He will also have wide powers to control the resources in both men and material within the County.

EMP/1551G/2, January 1986/JF, para 7, Kent County Council

Rather worryingly:

The County Controller will act independently if communications to the Zone Headquarters are disrupted and will take full responsibility for survival operations within the County until contact could be re-established.

EMP/1551G/2, January 1986/JF, para 8, Kent County Council

By the early 1980s, a myriad of structural types were employed as County Main, County Standby and District Controls, populated with well-meaning civil officials who had attended one- or two-day courses on emergency procedures and complemented with police and other service personnel. This is the level of government most people are familiar with; would you be happy with the head of your Council 'acting independently' in times of crisis?

S-RC 10.2, Hack Green, Cheshire. As with Kelvedon Hatch, Hack Green was an old Rotor-period semi-sunken bunker, converted in the early 1980s at a cost of over £20 million. The Government was fully aware that any protected site would be a target of attack in the early phases of any future conflict. To minimise the effects of over-pressure from nuclear or conventional blast, and to protect against napalm or flame-throwers, a series of guards were placed over any weak points on the structure. These are the metal plates visible to the left of the mast.

S-RC 10.2, Hack Green, Cheshire. A huge staff representing Government departments, comprising everything from the Department of the Environment through to the Inland Revenue, were provided for, although one can only guess at why the taxman had a seat.

Oxfordshire County Main, Woodeaton. From here, officials of the County Council would prepare for the worst. Situated five miles to the north-east of the city centre, this purpose-built bunker is no more than a slight rise in the ground. Responsible for a population of around 500,000, the staff faced co-ordinating emergency sanitation and feeding as well as the disposal of human remains in near-chaotic conditions.

Avon County Council Main, Bristol. Naturally, not all County Councils were enthusiastic about the prospects of nuclear war or having to expend resources planning for the day. In Bristol, the War Room at Flowers Hill, dating from the 1950s, was designated the County Main for a while. However, by 1981 Avon publicly declared itself a 'Nuclear Free Zone' and refused to implement any further war plans. Inwardly they did maintain a bunker at the Council House – just in case!

West Oxfordshire District Council, Witney. The Home Defence Review undertaken by the new Conservative government in 1980 sought to encourage councils to plan for Armageddon. The control at Witney is a good example of where your district councillors would attend to your wellbeing post-nuclear strike. The following five images show the Witney bunker.

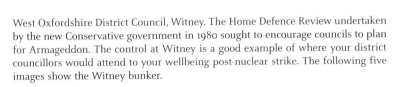

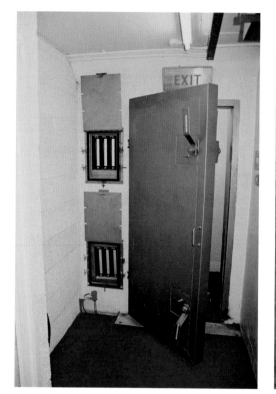

Above left: Blast doors capable of withstanding a substantial overpressure ensured relative safety once inside the bunker. This is the inner of two doors, the primary being around the corner. The vents on the left allow the pressure to be equalised before opening the door.

Above right: The capability to hold meetings was central to the function of the bunker. What is interesting is the drapery arranged in the room – behind it is a blank wall. Clearly, the stress of being underground for long periods would take its toll on the occupants.

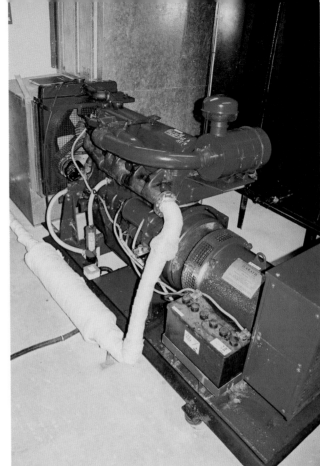

Above left: Fallout and chemical attack were as real a threat at a district level as they were at the big government sites, especially since most controls were not far from military establishments. This substantial filter would be slaved into the air-conditioning when an 'Air Attack Red' or 'Fallout Black' warning was given.

Above right: The control was self-sufficient in electricity for at least twenty-eight days straight. All bunkers had some form of generation unit to provide power for equipment and to run the air conditioning plant. Damage to the National Grid would mean most of the public would not experience electricity for many years to come.

This is the emergency exit of the Witney bunker. In peacetime, to use it, the occupants simply opened a blast door, ascended the steps and slid back the cover. During war, the whole step area would be filled with sand. If the council offices were destroyed, closing off the main entrance, then the occupants would have to be dug out – presuming anyone was available by that stage!

Chapter 8

THE PUBLIC

Protest

Britain's Cold War was punctuated from the mid-1950s by an heightened level of public opposition to both home-developed and American nuclear weapons. A number of civil action groups sprung up, including the 'Spies for Peace', intent on exposing secret sites, and 'The Direct Action Committee', a demonstration pressure group. However, the most famous and widespread was the Campaign for Nuclear Disarmament – CND – an organisation that continues to this day.

Opposition to nuclear weapons had started in 1952, but it was towards the end of the decade, in response to rapid changes in Government defence policy, that many felt forced into action. At the Bermuda Conference in 1957, agreement had been reached with the USA to base sixty Thor IRBMs along the east coast of Britain, whilst still developing Britain's own deterrent – the V-force. What incensed many was that whilst the missiles would be operated and maintained by the Royal Air Force under *Project Emily*, Washington had control of the warheads. In

February 1958, a launch meeting was held at the Conway Hall in London – the Campaign for Nuclear Disarmament (CND) was born. The following several seasons saw marches from London to Aldermaston and later the reverse, assembling at Aldermaston and then marching to a mass rally in Trafalgar Square.

By the early 1960s, the great crusade was in trouble. More notable figures, including actress Vanessa Redgrave, demanded wholesale disobedience to Parliament, as Bertrand Russell, one of the founding members, had initially intended. Russell resigned as CND President and formed the Committee of 100, who demanded protestors invade and occupy an area or site, defending their position using barricades. They should refuse to obey any order given by the police and allow themselves to be arrested without retaliation or violence. Focus drifted in the 1960s–70s to the Vietnam War, further damaging CND's profile. However, pressure was kept up at the Holy Loch submarine base, home of the Polaris.

With the announcement that American-controlled cruise missiles were to be stationed across Europe, including two sites in Britain, CND membership numbers dramatically increased. Protests against NATO's new nuclear framework spread across Europe. However, it was events at Greenham Common that attracted the most media attention, interestingly not organised by CND. The first peace camp started in late 1981 when a group, comprising mainly women, arrived on a march from Cardiff. The camps came to symbolise not only the struggle against nuclear weapons but also the perceived view that nuclear war was a male-dominated environment. The Government took a dim view of the situation and it wasn't long before key members of the Greenham Women were under surveillance by both police and MI5. Periodically, evictions were carried out, often ending in violence, damaging the Government's position and strengthening the protesters' resolve in the process. It has been hinted that the group was infiltrated by Soviet operatives as well as British, but this is yet to be substantiated.

The protest against the deployment of cruise missiles was both static and mobile. GLCMs were designed to be deployed well away from the parent site; the problem was, CND had other ideas. As the launchers left Greenham Common on exercise they became prime targets for the protesters. To exploit this highly visible form of protest, a network was set up called 'Cruise Watch', aimed at tracking the convoys and causing as many problems in transit as possible. This caused a major headache for the security services, making the convoys anything other than discreet. The situation became so bad that deployments had to be undertaken in the early hours and protected by a massive civilian and MOD police presence. Blockades were set up, occasionally causing accidents, and deployment sites such as MOD Boscombe Down soon sprouted their own 'mini' peace camps. But it was at Greenham Common that the large protests, so typifying the Cold War, were played out in front of the world's media.

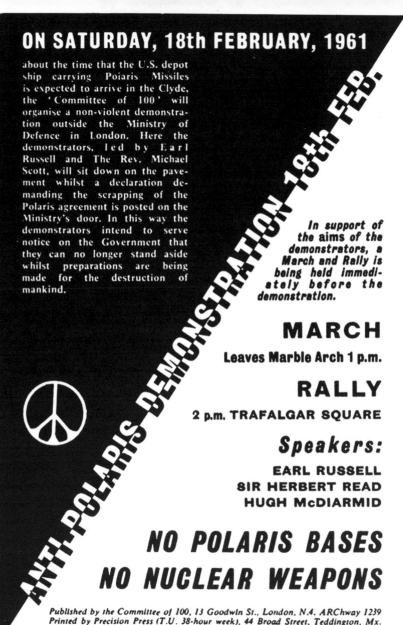

Above left: Aldermaston March, 1963. Over the 1958 Easter holiday, the first of many peace marches made their way from a rally in Trafalgar Square to the AWRE Aldermaston. There they were met by thousands of other protesters. The majority were well-educated, middle-class individuals, far removed from traditional political activists, leading Tony Benn, in 1963, to comment, 'They were a nice, keen crowd, though mainly middle-class – one of CND's greatest weaknesses.'

Above right: Hiroshima has proven the staple diet for all nuclear protestors and featured as heavily as the CND symbol in any march or demonstration. That the United States has been the only nation to use nuclear weapons in war made the use of the city's name so poignant to British protesters.

Opposite: The Committee of 100. This poster calls for participation in an anti-Polaris march and rally in Trafalgar Square. The Campaign for Nuclear Disarmament symbol (lower left on this poster) was designed by Gerald Holton in the late 1950s. It has been interpreted as showing a broken cross but is more likely the semaphore signals for the letters N and D. Holton refused to copyright the symbol, saying it should be freely available. The symbol is now as much a fashion statement as a political one.

Above: The first peace protestors arrived at RAF Greenham Common in late 1981. It was soon established as a women-only venture due to the perceived view that nuclear war was a male-dominated environment. CND distanced itself from the camps; however, the KGB did not and it is rumoured that the site was infiltrated by Soviet agents. (Department of Defense Imagery photo no. DF-ST-84-08474)

Right: RAF Molesworth. Molesworth was to become the second UK station to receive the cruise missile systems. The site did not attract as much publicity as Greenham Common, primarily because it was a CND-focused protest. In this 'call-to-protest' in 1984, the demonstrators hoped to dissuade the Government by using the environmental angle. RAF Molesworth never reached nuclear capability as the Intermediate-range Nuclear Forces (INF) treaty in 1987 banned the use of the cruise missile.

MOLESWORTH the second Greenham?

THE DECISION TO BASE CRUISE AT MOLESWORTH When NATO decided to place 10 flights of cruise missiles on British soil, six of these were destined for Greenham Common and four for Molesworth in Cambridgeshire. Each flight consists of four launchers, 16 missiles, and control vehicles.

THE SITE RAF Molesworth is an 800 acre disused airfield. It is, at the moment, an area of open grassland in the heart of the countryside. It is unfenced and unused—except as a centre for peace activities. To build the base they will have to start from scratch. Work is due to start in February 1985. But before that the Ministry of Defence will have to erect a high security fence around the area. Surveying for this has already begun. They may start **putting up the fence at any moment**.

DEFEND MOLESWORTH We have a unique opportunity to resist the military invasion of a piece of English countryside—**before** the building begins. We can non-violently resist the seizing, enclosing and desecration of this grassland. We do so in the name of the great majority of British people who oppose the building of a second cruise base in this country.

The Pledge

CND is calling for non-violent resistance to the construction work at Molesworth. A national rota is being set up to ensure that the peace movement has a significant and continuing presence at the site. To join this rota you do not have to commit yourself to civil disobedience—other supporting roles are vital to successful action.

Details of the pledge and the rota are on the reverse side of this leaflet. There is a pledge form to fill in and send off.

Pledge NOW To Defend Molesworth

Defend Molesworth

Against Cruise NOW

Above: A message from the security fence at RAF Greenham Common to President Reagan in 1983. (Photograph by Sigrid Møller. The Danish Peace Academy)

Left: The security fence at RAF Greenham Common was under constant attack from the protesters. Outside the wire the local police force had jurisdiction, inside it was the uniformed services who guarded the site. (Department of Defense Imagery photo no. DF-ST-84-08382)

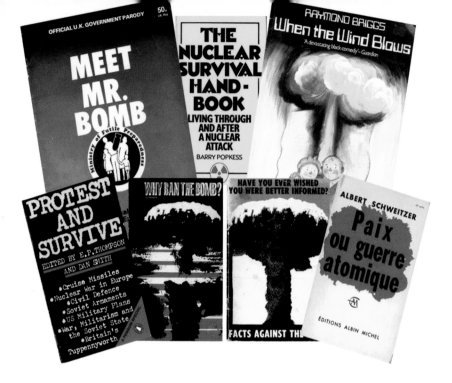

Publications on the apocalypse naturally appeared on the shelves and ranged across the whole spectrum of public opinion. Themes were diverse: *When the Wind Blows* by Raymond Briggs, better known for *The Snowman* than nuclear war, presented a dark post-nuclear world whilst Barry Popkess schooled the public on survival techniques. Others simply poked fun at the futility of it all! (Covers various, Arrow and Penguin)

Blockading the gates. As the protests at RAF Greenham Common dragged on and the level of civil disobedience grew, the press were never far away. Every time the protesters were evicted or caused a disturbance, the events were flashed around the world, gathering more support. (Photograph by Sigrid Møller. The Danish Peace Academy)

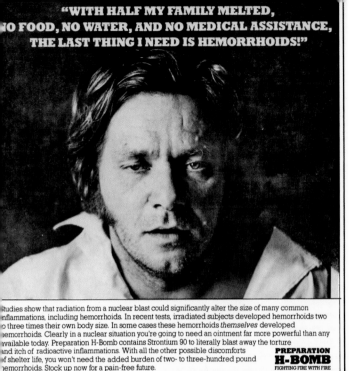

Above left: Fatalist comedy had two main directions: the general warmongering appearance of the political leaders and their apparent race towards Armageddon, impressively chronicled weekly throughout the 1980s by *Spitting Image*; and the plight of the public, including the inevitability of 'when the bomb drops', often asking 'what would you do with your four minutes?'

Above right: Naturally, the Cold War and nuclear weapons found their way into the very fabric of British life. Beyond Ian Fleming and the exploits of 007 came such novels as *On the Beach* by Nevil Shute, where survivors of a devastated world struggle to come to terms with death through the effects of radiation. Similar horrors were visited by the BBC with the drama *Threads* in 1984. Meanwhile, 'Frankie' and Blondie hit the charts, as did Orchestral Manoeuvres in the Dark, with 'Enola Gay'. (ZTT, Dindisc and Chrysalis /EMI)

Above left: The Civil Defence Corps. Spurred on by events in Berlin, the British Government passed the Civil Defence Act (1948), making provision for the protection of the public against attack from overseas. By April 1949, this had led to the creation of a voluntary service – the Civil Defence Corps (CDC). Primary tasks of the CDC were Headquarters, Rescue, Warden, Welfare and Ambulance. The organisation survived until swingeing defence cuts in 1968 led to the CDC being disbanded.

Above right: Atomic Cities. The Civil Defence Corps was the responsibility of the County Councils, reimbursed by Central Government through the Home Office. The authority recruited and trained volunteers and maintained facilities and equipment. Training centres were specially built, known locally as 'Atomic Cities', where members were schooled in the art of rescue in hazardous conditions.

Above: Civil Defence Literature. To assist in the correct running of the CDC, the Government issued a comprehensive range of handbooks and leaflets – not all were intended for public release.

Right: In 1951 a new wing of the CDC was formed – The Industrial Civil Defence Service (ICDS). All companies employing 200 or more people would establish a civil defence regime. Staff were trained in first aid, fire fighting and light rescue. Interestingly this formed the basis of much staff training we recognise today. An exercise at Cross Hands Steel Works, Tin Plate Division, Wales, in the early 1960s is seen here.

Above: CDC Equipment. To function properly the CDC was provided with a range of vehicles, some specialist, some questionable. Effective communications would be critical to CDC operations post-attack and many teams were specifically tasked with maintaining or running signals. Each echelon contained a mobile signals office such as this Fordson Thames Trader conversion.

Right: Much of the United Kingdom's telephone network was supported on poles during the Cold War. Naturally this was very susceptible to blast, nuclear or otherwise, so a viable cable laying division was needed. Equipped to repair overhead cables or deploy additional ground based lines, this is where the Field Cable Party came into its own.

Quite how an open-top bus would be used in fallout conditions is anybody's guess! It is more likely that this vehicle was used at recruitment drives. In the period 1953–54, almost 500,000 were in uniform but with the realisation that war with the H-bomb was an unmanageable event, membership steadily dropped off.

Column Rescue Vehicle (CRV). The CRV, manned by a crew of eight, carried a wide range of equipment including oxy-acetylene cutting equipment and lifting and shoring kit. After an attack, the CRV would make its way back into the devastated area with the intention of rescuing those who were trapped in the wreckage.

AFTER a hydrogen bomb attack, thousands would be homeless, hungry, exhausted and frightened. Help and comfort would come from the Welfare Section. Its members are training now for such tasks as evacuation and reception, emergency feeding, and running rest centres, information centres and mobile canteens.

An Emergency Feeding Unit with an improvised hot-plate cooker.

8

THE H-BOMB
What about the millions of survivors?

CIVIL DEFENCE
is common sense

Above left and right: Surviving the H-Bomb. One of the major selling points of the CDC was its Welfare Section. Care and billeting of the homeless, field kitchens, keeping children occupied and maintaining a level of basic human needs, especially when it came to ablutions, were all part of the remit. However, H-bomb warfare was completely different to that of the atomic bomb and these services, run in the main by well-meaning ladies 'of a certain age', would have been quickly overrun.

Above: Auxiliary Fire Service (AFS) Green Goddess. The Civil Defence Act (1948) demanded a fire-fighting service autonomous of the local authority brigades and, in November 1949, the Auxiliary Fire Service (AFS) was reformed. Initially equipped with war-surplus pumps and appliances, in 1953 it took delivery of a new pump, one of the most enduring symbols of the Cold War. Manned by a crew of six, it was painted AFS dark green to identify it from local authority red appliances. The Green Goddess was born.

Right: Women's Voluntary Service (WVS). The WVS had its roots in the immediate pre-war build-up of services in the United Kingdom. It took its Civil Defence role very seriously and had staff working at all levels of the organisation, tending to the welfare of those who were in turn caring for the public. The WVS issued its own information leaflet on nuclear attacks and curiously outlived all other services, being involved in staff welfare in nearly all bunkers up to Regional Seat level until the end of the Cold War.

INDICATIONS OF DANGER

BEFORE ATTACK

FIRST STAGE
There would be an official instruction to take precautions.

SECOND STAGE
Our warning system is designed to provide a warning before an attack reaches this country, giving enough time to get under cover.

DURING ATTACK

The light from a nuclear explosion would warn those not under cover to seek instant protection against the other possible dangers – heat, blast, radioactive fall-out.

AFTER ATTACK

Warnings would be given to those places which fall-out was approaching.

Civil Defence post-1968

With the stand-down of the CDC, all aspects of help for the public during a national emergency were downgraded. Over the subsequent decade, Central Government did little beyond publishing information leaflets but there was to be no trained body to oversee the coordination of the survivors. A large proportion of the equipment amassed over the previous twenty years was disposed of, while what was left would be controlled by the Regional Commissions. In 1980, Margaret Thatcher initiated a review of all civil protection, setting the scene for a new wave of spending. In 1981, the Home Office announced that funding would be aimed at local authorities, destined to become the front line of Civil Defence, with grants for a new post – the Emergency Planning Officer (EPO). National training courses were set up at Easingwold for the EPO who was then, again with Central Government funding, to run courses for local authority staff. Whilst this was being set up, the Government went on the 'charm offensive', underpinning why the United Kingdom needed to maintain a credible deterrent. Unfortunately, the public would still have to shoulder the majority of a nuclear attack and its aftermath alone.

Above: During the 'Doom Boom' of the late 1970s and early 1980s, the Government, through various departments, sought to convince the public that the British deterrent was essential to their way of life. A series of leaflets was freely distributed across the country in an attempt to justify defence expenditure – £12.3 billion or 5.2 per cent of GDP in 1981/82 – and the poor track record of the Soviet leadership in arms reductions. (© Crown Copyright)

Left: In 1976, the Government published one of the most controversial leaflets of the Cold War – *Protect and Survive*. Naturally, anti-nuclear groups had a field day. Accompanying it was a series of short films narrated, ironically, by the voice of Barratt Homes – Patrick Allen. Everything from conserving drinking water by tying up the toilet handle to where to bury family members was covered. A number of other leaflets were published at the same time but they never achieved such notoriety. (© Crown Copyright)

At home

All at home must go to the fall-out room and stay inside the inner refuge, keeping the radio tuned for Government advice and instructions.

How *Protect and Survive* envisaged the 'nuclear' family entering their inner refuge for a minimum of fourteen days. It is worth studying what this author considers to be one of the darkest images of Britain's Cold War. The illustrator (unknown at present) unwittingly portrays the inevitability of the family's situation through the body language of the parents and older child. (© Crown Copyright)

Protect and Survive's optimism was often ridiculed, especially when it advised: *On hearing the All-Clear: This means there is no longer an immediate danger from air attack and fallout and you may resume normal activities.*

Regional Government did not share the optimism, noting in contemporary Civil Protection courses through the 1980s: *It might be necessary to resort to mass burials or cremation.* Whoever occupied this seat during a nuclear exchange would soon appreciate the true meaning of Armageddon!

Chapter 9

WHAT NEXT?

It is now just over twenty years since the Berlin Wall was breached and the start of the end for the Soviet regime, which too had gone by 25 December 1991. The 'Peace Dividend' immediately made a huge dent in the United Kingdom's defence infrastructure. This, coupled with later cost-saving initiatives, has ensured the current armed forces are less than half the strength of twenty years ago. The whole network of bunkers and associated infrastructure had been disposed of by 1996, something many are now questioning.

The Cold War is now accessible to the public at a number of locations. Most aircraft museums boast an exhibit or two from the period and an increasing number contain nuclear weapons – decommissioned, I hasten to add! Beyond provincial collections, a number of sites do warrant specific mention.

The number of USAF-operated stations in the United Kingdom was also re-assessed with the collapse of the Soviet Union. By the mid-1980s US principal airfields in Britain included Alconbury, Bentwaters, Fairford, Greenham Common, Lakenheath, Mildenhall, Molesworth, Upper Heyford and Woodbridge. In addition, Sculthorpe, Wethersfield and Boscombe Down were designated reserve stations with maintenance being undertaken on F-111s and A-10s at Filton and Kemble respectively. A number of USAF squadrons quickly deployed to the Gulf as part of 'Desert Shield', later 'Desert Storm' and were stood down from there.

And so the Cold War was replaced by a hot one in the sands of the Arabian Peninsula. Now the threats are international terrorism and extremism, harboured by rogue states. Governments tell us the stakes are high, the fabric of our very way of life is under threat and we must see through the stabilisation of Afghanistan. Remember there has only ever been one nuclear war: it lasted three days and they used every weapon they had. Thankfully, that was in 1945. Now the world watches as Iran blatantly ignores international opinion, North Korea conducts tests and Pakistan, a major nuclear power, teeters on the edge of extremism. Clearly, things have the potential to get a lot hotter over the coming decades.

Removal of Fylingdales' 'Golf balls'. Irrespective of their cult status, the 'golf balls' at RAF Fylingdales were cleared to make way for a new surveillance system. The problem is the Four Minute Warning would be totally wasted on a Britain now unprepared for nuclear war. (Courtesy of *Scarborough Evening News*)

Go in, Stay in, Tune in, 2004. In the wake of the renewed terrorist threats and attack on the United States, the Government issued a booklet entitled *Preparing for Emergencies*. Naturally, it was compared with *Protect and Survive* but crucially the new booklet did not mention war. (© Crown Copyright)

Opposite: XH558 photographed over RAF Marham in 1992. This Vulcan is now the world's only flying example of a 'V' Force aircraft. (Courtesy of Adrian Balch)

Above left: Hack Green Nuclear Bunker. The country's finest collection of Cold War artefacts.
Info Line: 01270 629219
Administration: 01270 623353
Fax: 01270 629218
Email: coldwar@hackgreen.co.uk
PO Box 127
Nantwich
Cheshire, CW5 8AQ

Above right: Kelvedon Hatch. The country's most original Cold War display.
Kelvedon Hatch Secret Nuclear Bunker
Telephone: 01277 364883
Email: bunkerinfo@japar.demon.co.uk
Crown Buildings
Kelvedon Hall Lane
Kelvedon Hatch
CM14 5TL